So You Want to Coach
Girls' Lacrosse

So You Want to Coach
Girls' Lacrosse

Richard H. Shriver

WHALER
BOOKS

Buena Vista, VA

1 3 5 7 9 10 8 6 4 2

Library of Congress Control Number: 2025900802

So You Want to Coach Girls' Lacrosse
Richard H. Shriver

p. cm.

1. Sports & Recreation: Lacrosse
2. Sports & Recreation: Coaching—Lacrosse
3. Sports & Recreation: Women in Sports

I. Shriver, Richard H., 1933– II. Title.

ISBN 13: 978-1-966392-01-9 (softcover : alk. paper)

Design and Layout by Karen Bowen

Inside back cover: This painting is by Bruce Macdonald who painted it for his friend, Dick Shriver, for inclusion in this book.

Whaler Books
An imprint of

Mariner Media, Inc.
131 West 21st Street
Buena Vista, VA 24416
Tel: 540-264-0021
www.marinermedia.com

Printed in the United States of America

This book is printed on acid-free paper meeting the requirements of the American Standard for Permanence of Paper for Printed Library Materials.

For Barb

and the

Women's Varsity Lacrosse Teams,
US Coast Guard Academy, 2008–2011

Williams School Girls' Varsity Lacrosse Teams,
2012–2014

Lyme Ticks Girls' Youth Teams,
2015–2017

Old Saybrook High School
Girls' Varsity Lacrosse Teams, 2018–2024

Acknowledgments

Hillary Sigersmith kept score as a
volunteer during two full seasons.

Joe Maselli devoted much time and skill to
create and curate the many photographs in this book.

Denise Dobratz read early drafts,
providing critique and helpful guidance.

Rich Shriver edited early content and provided
much encouragement to complete this book.

Kendall Dobratz, Julia Maselli, and Gretchen Kawecki
posed for the training photos in the book.

With Great Respect and Admiration

Bob Hulburd (Coach, 1947–1951)

Clancy Fauntleroy (Teammate, 1953–1955)

Kendall Hartt (Player and Captain, 2018)

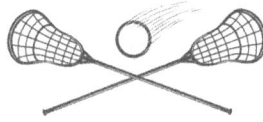

Table of Contents

Preface

We were barely three minutes into a game against North Branford, perennially one of our toughest competitors in the Shoreline League of Connecticut, and were already trailing by 0–3. An exasperated midfielder on our team, Ayla D'Anna, shouted to me as she headed back for the center draw following our opponents' third successive goal, "Coach, when is Maddie coming in?" Maddie was Madeline Beaudoin, a co-captain, who had been detained at school for an AP exam and had arrived at the game just after it started. I told Maddie to warm up and tell me when she was ready because I wanted her to go straight in. I turned around to check, and there she was on the bench while Briana, our second-string goalie, finished braiding Maddie's hair. I shouted back to Ayla, "She's almost ready."

Such is lacrosse in the smaller schools. We (the Old Saybrook High School Girls' Varsity Lacrosse Team) rarely started a season with a full team of twelve girls, all of whom could pass and catch under pressure. For my first five seasons as head coach at Old Saybrook, we typically had 18–19 players total, with 6 or 7 who were younger, less experienced, and best able to play at the junior varsity level. We had so little depth that missing a single player like Maddie could make an outsized difference. When necessary, which was most of the time, we expected our starting twelve to play for the entire 48 minutes without a substitution.

The above anecdote involving Maddie and North Branford took place in the 2023 season of the Shoreline Girls' Lacrosse League, a game that Old Saybrook managed to win, and a season in which our team won the league Championship.

This book is about the large group of average-to-small schools that are a part of the 3,000 Girls' Varsity High School Teams in the US with nearly 100,000 players. This is about those teams that don't always make it into state playoffs, typically have one or two players that make first- or second-team all-conference, and every now and then field a player who makes all-state…teams that struggle to field a competitive team each spring…teams that can do better by the season's end as their new, younger players catch on and begin to excel at the sport…teams whose parents care a lot about their daughters who are engaged in a sport they love, but that few of their parents knew about when they were in school.

Old Saybrook has such a team in that category, and it was a great pleasure and privilege for me to become their head coach. This was a position I filled from 2018 through the spring of 2024 when, at 90, I no longer had the stamina to do the job properly. Three weeks after I resigned from my coaching position, I was in the hospital with an array of issues, one set of which resulted in a new pacemaker. Some of my old stamina began to return, and for a brief period, I thought I may have resigned prematurely. No, it was time for me to retire…maybe I could write a useful book focusing on the 2024 season, my sixth at Old Saybrook as head coach. The book could incorporate what I had learned as a player of lacrosse for almost 20 years, and what I had learned as a coach of men's, women's, boys', girls', and youth teams over more than 20 years.

I was extremely fortunate to be head coach at Old Saybrook High School from 2018 through 2024 (we did not play in the spring of 2020 due to COVID). I understood that around the first week of March in 2018, the head coach of the Old Saybrook Girls' Varsity Lacrosse Team quit unexpectedly, with the season's start just days away. A friend, Tom Kehlenbach, father of Allie who was first-string attack on the team, told the Old Saybrook athletic director that he would like to coach the team, an offer that Mike Cunningham, the athletic director, turned down because Tom was the parent of a player. Tom then said, "Why don't you call Dick Shriver?" I had coached Allie in the regional youth program (The Lyme Ticks).

I had learned much about the girls' and women's games in earlier years.

In the spring of 2008, I was asked to be assistant coach of the Women's Lacrosse Team at the US Coast Guard Academy. This invitation came at the instigation of the advisor to the Women's Lacrosse Team, Anne Flammang, Captain, US Coast Guard (Retired). Lacrosse was a minor sport at the Academy at the time. This was my first experience with the female version of a sport I had first played in the spring of 1942. From 2009 through 2011, I was head coach of this team. After the Coast Guard Academy, I was hired as head coach of the Girls' Varsity Lacrosse Team at the Williams School, a private school in New London, CT. I coached this team for three years. By the spring of 2018, however, I was 84 years old with no reasonable prospect of another coaching job as important and as demanding as being head coach of a high school team. That is until Tom Kehlenbach recommended me.

Mike Cunningham asked if I would accept a position as "Emergency Head Coach," a state of CT designation that enabled a school to hire a coach without a normal search and without having to fulfill all of the state requirements for background checks and so on. The proviso: an emergency coach has no right to continue at the season's end. As it happened, our team did pretty well during the spring of 2018 and Old Saybrook invited me to apply to the state to be certified as a full-fledged head coach of Girls' Varsity Lacrosse.

Girls' Varsity Lacrosse is one of the hot spots in high school sports today. The sport is growing fast, there are many college scholarship opportunities with some at the high end, and the Women's Professional Lacrosse League is providing a few longer-term early career opportunities. Importantly, these champions are great role models for thousands of younger players. With nearly 20,000 high schools in the country and a Girls' Lacrosse Program in just 3,000 of them, it could be a long time before the country is saturated with Girls' High School Varsity Lacrosse Teams.

Along the way, thousands of girls in hundreds of schools will play on teams just like the Old Saybrook team of 2024, a year in which we had one senior and just fifteen names on the roster with no prospect of fielding a junior varsity team. This book is written for those girls, their teams, and their parents and coaches.

Chapter 1

The 2024 Girls Varsity Lacrosse Team, Old Saybrook HS, CT

Fifteen girls registered for the 2024 team, the same 15 girls showed up for the first practice, and the same 15 girls ended the season together. This should not be a big surprise, but the results of any season can be affected by the number of players and the stability of the team. If we had had fewer than 15, for example, or if one or two had quit, I think we would have had difficulty generating and maintaining the level of enthusiasm that was attained. Also, in the one game when we only had 11 players show up, against non-league New Fairfield, we would have played with even more players short of a full team and would have been humbled by an even more lopsided score.

Fifteen was the fewest number of players I had ever coached save for the first year of lacrosse at Mountain Lakes (NJ) in 1974 when we had thirteen. The gap occurred after the COVID season of 2020 when we didn't play, and we wound up with one player (Amelia Sigersmith) as the lone freshman during the 2021 season.

In our league, when teams with only 6 or 7 JV players were up against opponents who had more players, the latter team would scale back so that each team had the same number of players on the field. Such games were invaluable for experience and playing time for the more junior players. In 2024, with just 15, we had no chance to field a

Figure 1: The Official Team Roster for 2024

PLAYER	AGE	GRADE	JERSEY NR
Goalies			
Cali Morelli	17	11	11
Erin Fiorelli*	16	11	18
The Three Rotating Starters on Defense			
Felicia Lombard*	14	10	5
Julia Maselli*	14	10	13
Caroline Adams*	14	9	14
The Defense Cohort (Plus One of the Rotating Starters)			
Grace Desmond	17	11	7
Zoe Parakilas*	15	9	19
Emma Courtright*	15	10	10
The Attack Cohort			
Claire Courtright* **	14	9	3
Lila Cadley	17	11	1
Ainsley Sigersmith*	15	9	15
Sylvie Webber*	14	9	12
The Midfield Cohort (The "Draw Demons")**			
Amelia Sigersmith	17	12	16
Kendall Dobratz	16	10	17
Ayla D'Anna**	16	11	8

*   Players new to the team in 2024 (9)

**   At center draws, Claire lined up on attack while Ayla lined up at midfield for the center draw (Ayla, Amelia, and Kendall); after the draw, Claire and Ayla switched positions.

JV team. This was unfortunate for the 3 or 4 players who would have benefitted from the opportunity.

With 9 players new to the game at the high school level, it would not have been a surprise if we had lost 1 or 2 players precisely because we couldn't provide them with the JV experience. We worked extra hard to maintain their interest, but in the end, I believe they all enjoyed the social aspects of being on this team, and I doubt that any of them gave a thought to quitting. This was a credit to our captains who kept the morale high for the entire season.

The Goalies

Cali Morelli. Cali was (and, certainly, still is) an all-around athlete. As our first-string goalie the previous year, she was ready to excel this season. By the same token, Cali was also a champion cheerleader during the fall and winter seasons, and in the spring, she was invited to participate in cheerleading events around the country for recognition and awards (She could do a backflip from a standing position). These events conflicted somewhat with her own objectives for the lacrosse season, but she did well and will have another season as a senior in 2025.

Erin Fiorelli. Erin joined the team in 2024 with little lacrosse experience, but plenty of goalie experience in another sport. Once Erin learned how to pass with her goalie stick, one of the more difficult skills to master, her lacrosse career was sealed. Well into the season, Erin started in the goal when Cali was away. She held her own against our worthiest adversaries.

The Three Rotating Starters at Defense

The starting team of 12 included 11 players whose positions were relatively assured. This left one position to be filled by any one of the three newcomers, freshman Caroline Adams or either of the two sophomores, both new to high school lacrosse, Julia Maselli and Felicia (Flea) Lombard. We elected to start with all of our more experienced players at midfield and attack; this left the one open starting position on defense.

Caroline Adams. Caroline came with experience in youth lacrosse. Her older sister, Grace, had been a captain of the varsity team in 2023, so she had the advantage of a mentor within her family (Her mother, Katie, had also played lacrosse). As the season progressed, so did Caroline. The leader of our defense, Grace Desmond, often asked us to send Caroline in as she had become quite proficient in guarding her opponent and was increasingly helpful in running out clears.

Julia Maselli. Julia joined the team in 2024, having had prior experience in youth lacrosse. She progressed well during the season, playing on attack as often as defense. Given her height and interests, the best position for Julia in the future will likely be attack. Her positive attitude in all situations will serve her well.

Felicia (Flea) Lombard. Flea joined the team in 2024 also with experience in youth lacrosse. While she played on defense for much of the 2024 season, her longer-term aspirations and capabilities probably lie in the attacking zone. It's just a matter of time as her speed, stickhandling, and confidence in combat develop.

The Defensive Cohort

The 2024 defense was led by Grace Desmond, a junior, plus three girls all new to the team in 2024. The other three defenders included Emma Courtright, Zoe Parakilas, and alternating, one of the three starter substitutes, Julia, Flea, or Caroline.

Grace Desmond. Grace joined the team as a freshman in 2022. She was such a good stick-handler that she initially played attack. At one point, we asked her to try defense where she excelled. In 2024, Grace was co-captain and leader of the defensive cohort. This was no small task as the others in her cohort were the least experienced players on the team. This was a conscious decision by the coaches as our "game plan" for the season was to get the ball at the draw, hang on to it, score, and then repeat…i.e., we wanted to deny our opponents opportunities to score in the first place. This strategy worked against most of our league opponents. When playing the toughest teams, we often put one, or even two, of the more experienced players in on defense. Among Grace's great strengths was her ability to lead the defensive cohort by example, generally taking the most critical scoring areas for herself. Under Grace's leadership, the defense created a "wall" of players, sliding quickly to the most threatening opponent, making it as difficult as possible for opponents to get off a decent shot. Moreover, with her excellent stick-handling ability, Grace could clear the ball into our attacking zone by herself.

Zoe Parakilas. We started Zoe as the number 2 defense player backing up Grace, and never changed during the season. Zoe had the athleticism and good team instincts that served her and her team well. Backing

up Grace meant Zoe's main job was to turn back the "stars" on the opposing teams if they were getting ahead of Grace. The teamwork between Grace and Zoe worked well as they frustrated many scoring attempts by our opponents.

Emma Courtright. Emma was a steady performer on defense throughout the 2024 season. Joining the team in 2024 as a sophomore, Emma was a steady, reliable player. Emma learned how to place herself strategically between the girl she was guarding and the threats from others who might break into the clear. Emma lived by the rule, "you can never slide too soon," as she managed to get in the face of our worthiest opponents at the right time.

The Attack Cohort

Lila Cadley. As a junior, this was Lila's third year on our team. She had demonstrated her capacity for competitive play in the prior seasons, and I felt 2024 was going to be a big year for Lila. It was. Lila could get pretty excited in the ferocity of close combat around the goal; in the 2024 season, she channeled her emotions into positive outcomes for her team. I enjoyed being Lila's coach as much as anyone I ever coached.

Claire Cassella. Even though Claire joined the team as a freshman, after the first practice it seemed as if she had been on the team forever. Claire had great experience in youth lacrosse and had excelled at the

game before high school. With excellent stick-handling and dodging skills, Claire added much to the scoring power of our team. Claire's most impressive attribute was her innate ability to know where to be on the field at all times to be most helpful to her team.

Sylvie Webber. There was really no other logical position for Sylvie than attack, behind the goal…preferably on the left side. This afforded her the best opportunities to roll the crease. As a freshman, Sylvie showed up having had much good experience before high school. Sylvie possessed good stick-handling and dodging capabilities but needed to develop her confidence at the high school level in taking offensive risks. As that self-confidence gained momentum during the season, Sylvie contributed to the team's performance in significant ways.

Ainsley Sigersmith. Ainsley was the fourth of four Sigersmith sisters that I was privileged to coach at Old Saybrook. All were accomplished athletes and cheerful but formidable competitors. Ainsley joined the team as a freshman in 2024, certainly in no small part because her older sister, Amelia, was co-captain. Her favorite sport was soccer, so we were lucky to have her on the 2024 team. She was tall and had excellent stick-handling skills, so she was logically placed behind the goal at attack, on the right. In 40-yard sprints, however, Ainsley was always out in front…easily. Given her ability to control the ball in combat, we sent Ainsley in at defense to help with clears. If she got the ball in the defensive zone, she could outrun and out-dodge opponents, clearing the ball the length of the field. Hopefully, she enjoyed the 2024 season sufficiently to continue with lacrosse throughout high school.

Midfield

This cohort was key to our game during the 2024 season. We put the three most aggressive, most experienced players, our best stick-handlers at the center draw. Their job was to "get the ball." We called them our "Draw Demons." They were all outstanding on ground balls, managing to pluck the ball out of any mayhem. Against the teams in our league, the Draw Demons never got less than 50%, sometimes as high as 70% or 80%. This lineup proved to be the most successful of our strategies for 2024.

Amelia Sigersmith. Amelia was co-captain and our lone senior on the team. It was my sixth season as Amelia's coach, four in high school and two in the youth league. Amelia's long suits included the litany of stick-handling skills, ground balls, passing and catching under pressure, controlling the ball, and making plays from the midfield. Amelia had poise. If we had measured assists over the seasons, Amelia would certainly have had a school record for the number of assists during her career as a high school player. Amelia displayed great leadership and sportsmanship by example at all times. She can look back on her lacrosse career with great pride in how she managed herself and contributed to her team's accomplishments.

Ayla D'Anna. Ayla exemplified the adage, "Be your best when you have to be your best." She thrived on the field of gritty combat. She was fast, wily, and managed to get in position for a shot at the goal almost at will. Ayla had strong personal goals such as "career goals scored" which she cheerfully subordinated to the priorities of her

team. As a co-captain of the 2024 team in her junior year, she excelled at getting off shots at the goal. She invented a dodge from behind the goal with an effective backhand shot at the goalie's feet that befuddled our opponents (and me). Opponents feared her. One time in the 2023 season, with the score tied and seconds to go, Ayla had a free-position penalty shot at the 8-meter arc. Cool as a cucumber, she fired off the winning goal.

Kendall Dobratz. Kendall was still a sophomore in 2024 but played far above her age. A superb and natural athlete, her favorite sport was ice hockey, a sport that took her to another school in 2025. On the lacrosse field, Kendall could be counted upon to think on her feet and do the right thing spontaneously. As a midfielder, Kendall was all over the field, on defense or attack or anywhere else. She had countless interceptions to her credit, she could clear the ball the length of the field, and she could score with her sidearm slap shot from the 8-meter line. Kendall's attitude toward the game, toward her team and her teammates, was exemplary in every way. Our opponents learned that Kendall could be dangerous anytime she had the ball in her stick. Kendall will be remembered at Old Saybrook as a model of good sportsmanship, fair play, always practicing hard and even when exhausted, exceptional performance every minute of every game.

The Co-Captains

The 2024 Girls' Varsity Lacrosse Team of Old Saybrook was fortunate to have three captains, one each on attack, defense, and midfield. They worked well together, had great respect for one another, and were universally respected by their teammates.

Amelia, Grace, and Ayla

The "Draw Demons": Amelia, Ayla, and Kendall

The Team

Back Row: Flea, Claire, Caroline, Zoe, Ainsley, Sylvie, Julia
Front Row: Erin, Cali, Emma, Kendall, Amelia, Ayla, Grace, Lila

Chapter 2
Working With What You Have
Building the Best Team for the
Five Functions of Team Lacrosse

Players arrive at the start of the season as either veterans or newcomers (such as freshmen). We knew the veterans well, what they could do, where they needed work, and what position they might best work into. For the 9 players new to the team in 2024, however, it was a time of uncertainty and indecision…not for them. For me. Six of them would be on the starting team! Which six, though, and in what positions?

This is one of the most creative and important times of the season. How to begin to structure the team? Leaving out the goalie position (we had two goalies, which left 13 other players), in our case, we had 11 positions to fill with 13 players.

In the smaller schools such as Old Saybrook, and to an extent in all schools, there is bound to be one position, possibly two, that the coach will feel is especially weak. The question is, where do you choose to be weak? Offense or defense? Or conversely, and putting a positive spin on things, where do you choose to be the strongest?

I believe most coaches focus on offense, and try to put the best team together to score goals. That's the easiest team to configure. I also like to think, "What's the best team we can assemble to deny the other team the most goals?" That is probably a different team. Most of the time, we fielded our best offensive team; there were times, however, when we deliberately fielded our best defensive team.

We start by laying out the five functions that a team must fulfill. Once we had the starting 12 for the first game, I would spend the rest of the season tinkering with individual positions. My indecision with regard to starters and their positions must have been frustrating to the players from time to time, but there were usually one or two positions still in question right up to the end of the season.

The five functions:

1. **GET THE BALL!**
2. **SCORE!**
3. **RIDING CLEARS:** Stop opponent's clearing attempts.
4. **DEFENDING:** Don't let them score.
5. **CLEARING:** Clear the ball from our end of the field to our attacking end.

As coaches, we try to determine who are the best players for each function, independent of their interests or prior positions played. Then we try to determine how best to allocate the players. Every now and then, for a specific game or situation during a game, we may decide to overload defense instead of offense, so we try to help the players involved remain fluid in their thinking and expectations. We assign specific players to three of the functions, get the ball, score, and defend; then we count on those players to learn how to clear (the defensive cohort) and how to ride the clear (the offensive cohort).

GET THE BALL!

Our first priority in 2024 was "Get the ball," not just ground balls, but expressly the center draw, which often devolves into a ground ball situation. For that, we already had from 2023 our midfield for the center draw, the Draw Demons, co-captains Amelia and Ayla, and sophomore Kendall Dobratz. All three were fearless when it came to ground balls, excellent stick handlers, and very competitive. Every one of them knew how to "scoop through" the crowd to get the ball. They made a great cohort. Amelia and Kendall played midfield after the draw, but Ayla played attack. After the draw, Ayla switched with freshman Claire who lined up on defense, but then joined the midfield.

SCORE!

In order to score a goal, one must be able to pass and catch and shoot under pressure. Not every member of the offense needs to be able to score, however. If a player on offense is not expected to shoot or score, she must at least be able to keep the ball in play. Having so few players, we often had on the offensive seven a player who could not shoot with enough speed or power or accuracy to score. Each year, it seems, I had one player, or at least a substitute, to whom I would say, "I want you to go in for so and so, but whatever you do, don't try to shoot. Your shot isn't strong enough," or "If you try to dodge through this crowd, they will tear you apart." No girl wants to hear those things, but a weak shot (or a broken dodge) from such a player is an almost certain turnover to the other team and an embarrassment for our player.

I try to prepare players in advance for what could be a difficult conversation; on the plus side, I'm letting her know that she's going to get in this game, albeit maybe for a short time, with certain restrictions and conditions. A few years earlier, we had one player, a senior who played starting attack. I asked her not to shoot, and for the whole season she passed and caught under pressure and the team was undefeated that year. I don't recall that she ever scored, but she started in every game and had some great assists; she did her part.

For the offensive seven in 2024, we needed three more players. Grace would have been the next best stick-handler under pressure and had been quite good at attack as a freshman, but had become a talented defensive player and was now the leader of our defensive cohort, so we ruled her out as a candidate. Thus, we were drawn to the next three best stick-handlers and experienced players.

Lila was an obvious choice. She loved the whole concept of attack and could run like the wind. She had played attack the previous two seasons and was getting better and better in this position. This could be a great year for Lila at attack. More of a runner than a dodger, Lila learned to control the ball under competitive fire to a degree I never really understood…mainly focus and determination, I think. Also through hard work, she had learned to catch absolutely anything thrown her way. I could not picture myself persuading Lila to play defense; we had put her there from time to time during previous seasons, but it was not her long suit. Lila would play attack this season.

Ainsley, a freshman, was tall and somewhat experienced having played youth lacrosse (Ainsley was also the youngest of four lacrosse-playing sisters, all of whom I had coached…senior and co-captain Amelia was her older sister); Ainsley's favorite sport, however, was soccer, the spring program for which intervened from time to time. While we may not have had Ainsley's full attention and dedication throughout the season, in games, we could rely on her to do her best.

In addition…Ainsley was fast. In practice, when we had sprints, Ainsley was always at the front…effortlessly, it seemed. She was generally tied with Kendall or Lila as the fastest player on the team.

For the most part, when Ainsley was with us, we put her in on attack. As she was left-handed, she played behind the goal on the right side. That way, she could do a crease roll and score from her strong side.

In a game against Morgan, though (Morgan was the high school for Clinton, CT; it was always a formidable foe, disciplined and well-coached), we were having great trouble clearing the ball from the defensive end. Out of frustration, I asked Ainsley to go in at defense. Before she went in, I said to her, "Ainsley, when you get the ball, I don't want you to pass it. I want you to hang on to it and run it to the other end of the field." Ainsley did exactly that. Five times she grabbed the ball at the defensive end and ran it, through thick and thin, to the other end…scoring twice. The next day, Ainsley didn't show up for practice. I heard later that her legs were too sore. Ainsley would be our sixth offensive player.

Sylvie, a junior but new to our team in 2024, rounded out our offensive cohort. Sylvie had played youth lacrosse and could handle herself in close-quarters scoring situations. At the season's start, though, I noticed that she often appeared to be in the right position for an assist, but her teammates, for some reason, wouldn't pass to her. Was that because her teammates lacked confidence in Sylvie, or because Sylvie lacked confidence in herself? We never had to answer this question as Sylvie's self-confidence improved steadily, enabling her to contribute to the team's success toward the season's end when it counted most.

RIDING: Stop the opponents from clearing

This is often a low priority with coaches. It was not so with my school in Baltimore in the 1940s, or my high school team. The goalie and the defensive cohort automatically have an extra player at that end of the field, and if they can all pass and catch reasonably well, there is not much the attacking cohort can do to stop them. But we practiced and scrimmaged this function. It is a drill wherein both sides can work to get better; the defense can work on clearing and the offense can work on stopping the clear during the same drill.

At our level of play, we would run up against attacking cohorts who thought the best way to stop the clearing team was to beat them with their sticks (I exaggerate, but not much), often with penalties for hitting or holding the player clearing the ball, or coming "too close" to the imaginary sphere around the head.

We tried to train our players that the best way to stop a defensive player running the ball downfield was by getting their bodies in front of the runner; if you can't get there and stay there, then she's gone, and it's best to let her go. It's not worth the penalty…or worse, the angst of injuring an opponent.

When I coached the Coast Guard women's team, one of the captains was Samantha Gordon. I don't think Sam had played lacrosse before coming to the academy, so she didn't have the intrinsic skills that many of her teammates possessed. But she was fast on her feet, athletic, a confident leader among equals, and wonderfully coachable. She played midfield. She asked me after practice one day what she could do to be more helpful to the team. I thought about it, and that night, I wrote her a long email. In it, I suggested how she could position herself for interceptions when our opponents were trying to clear the ball. The trick is to bait the clearing passer…by staying far enough away from an obvious receiver so that the passer thinks she can make a safe pass, and then Sam could dart in for the interception. If I feared I may have overstepped my bounds in some way with this letter, such fears vanished the next day as Sam strode onto the field, and in full view of the entire team, gave me a giant hug.

DEFEND...Don't let them shoot, or don't let them get off a good shot, or force the opponents to shoot from as far away, or at the worst possible angle, from the goalie as possible.

This can often be the most important of the five functions. Games can be won with a strong defense and a less strong offense. It's a risky gamble, however, so we only rarely overloaded defense at the expense of offense, but we did do it; you can't let the other team think they can just run and dodge and shoot at will.

For our team in 2024, we needed four defenders for this cohort.

Grace was our lead defender, and we deferred to her or sought her advice on all matters relating to the defense (as assistant coach, my son, Rich, focused on the defense; in high school, he had played attack and goalie). Zoe stood out as the next defensive player in line. We felt Zoe and Grace could create the most effective barrier to would-be attackers.

On a fast break, for example, to get to the goal, they'd have to get past Grace in the first instance, who, with her stick extended out on one side (the direction the attacker was running), her free arm out on the other side, made herself into a very big obstacle to get around. Fast breakers would be deflected time and again by Grace, backed up by Zoe. Zoe came onto the scene knowing how to defend, with stutter steps and good field position, instinctively knowing when to slide away from her girl to help another teammate in danger of losing her girl.

If an opponent failed to get around Grace and Zoe, her best recourse was to veer away from the goal and pass off to a teammate. For the latter, we relied mainly on Emma. Emma had some prior experience in lacrosse and, as a sophomore, had an edge on wisdom, where to be, and when. She was steady and dependable.

During the entire season, we never had a permanent assignee to our fourth defender position, the final player to make up our starting team. We rotated three players through this position, Caroline, Julia, and

Flea. Even though they had the least experience with lacrosse, they all became proficient at marking up on the next most dangerous attacker, wherever she was. Caroline, with her speed, became especially effective in this position, while Julia and Flea also substituted for members of the attack during the season.

The crux of playing defense on our team was to know when to slide from the girl you were marking to the girl with the ball. We taught our defense, "You can never slide too soon." We drilled this concept relentlessly. It was one of the repeated sayings which by mid-season, everyone, myself included, grew tired of hearing.

If the feed or pass-off to a teammate worked, and the receiving girl was close to the crease, the last resort was our goalie.

Goalies are trained in the same way as the protection division of the United States Secret Service: stand up and take the bullet to protect the president. Don't duck or dodge. It takes a special person to do that. Good goalies will try to get any part of their stick or anatomy in the path of a shot. Great goalies will disregard their own safety in the process. If they can stop the ball, get it in their stick, and run and cradle safely out into the mob, and then pass safely to a teammate who can catch under pressure, there is little more you could ask for. Our goalies this year were Cali and Erin. Cali was a junior with good hand and eye coordination, good stickwork, good at communicating with her teammates, and a healthy desire to excel. In her first three high school seasons, she amassed 238 saves.

Erin was an accomplished goalie in field hockey, so she brought good skills, and good hand and eye coordination to the position. Passing with a goalie stick was not one of them, however, at the start of the season. Being a pessimist in such situations, I worried about how much she could learn in time to be our starting goalie for the two games when Cali would be away. Assistant coach, Rich, took on this challenge. By mid-season, Erin had become an effective, all-around player in the goal.

If the opponents' fast break ended without success, they would move to a settled offense, seven vs seven.

Though I tried it on a few occasions, we were never successful with a zone defense. I may have been part of the problem not having had a lifelong familiarity with two rules of girls' lacrosse, notably shooting space and the three-second rule. If a defender is in the critical scoring area for more than three seconds and is not within a stick's length of an opponent, the whistle can blow and the opponents get a free position. Also, if a defender is out of position and tries to get to a girl before she shoots, she must not approach the attacker by running at her in line with the goal behind her until she is within a stick's length of the attacker. The violation is called "shooting space." The defender can run at her to one side of the shooting alley for the attacker, but it's a judgment call for the referee. It's also a candidate for shenanigans whereby the attacker purposefully moves to put the defender in the shooting lane thereby drawing a penalty. Ideally, referees will see the shooting space and blow the whistle before the attacker shoots; in this case, the defender is penalized and the attacker gets a free-position penalty shot. If the attacker shoots anyway and hits the defender, that can be a penalty against the shooter. It's complicated, and we will say more about this later on.

Our defense has always been one-on-one, or "man-to-man." The defender guarding the girl with the ball is shouting, "On ball, on ball." This means that the two defenders on either side of her must be ready to slide into position to stop the girl with the ball should she decide to challenge and make a solo dash for the goal. As the ball is thrown around the circle, the defenders rotate with it, moving in and out to mark up on the girl with the ball or prepare to slide to the girl if she threatens.

Communication on defense is as important as being able to pass and catch. The goalie can generally see what's transpiring better than the individual players. Calling to her teammates, even by their first names, to tell them when to "crash" on an attacking player is essential. The defender "on ball" must concentrate on her girl, so her teammates to either side, but behind her, must constantly let her know where they are by shouting, "Got your back." A defensive cohort that communicates often, loudly, and well will do better than a defensive cohort that is silent.

In our league, each team might get several free position shots from the 8-meter arc, a kind of "mano a mano" between the shooter and the goalie. The shooter can shoot from the 8, or try to run and dodge for a shot at short range (or, if the situation warrants, pass to another player in a better position to shoot). Penalty shots can determine the outcome of a game. We practiced these shots, and defending against them, in nearly every practice session. The players on offense had to decide whether to take the long shot or try to run in and dodge their way to the goal. Only four or five of our offensive cohort could hope to score from 8 meters away. We tried to teach all of them how to run and dodge their way in for the short shot. From the defender's point of view, if one could just touch the shooter's stick en route to the goal, and not be penalized for having her stick too close to the shooter's head, that would usually be enough to deflect the shot away from the goal.

When taking the long shot, the question is, do you try to hit a piece of white net with a straight shot in the air, or do you bounce it? A constant chant from the coaches was, "The bounce shot is twice as likely to go in as you think."

When we had a player out on a penalty, the other team had the "extra man." For us, this was really little different from regular 7 v 7 play. One of our players was the defender "on ball," with another defender on each side, also playing one on one, but ready to slide. The "extra man" was always 180 degrees away halfway around the circle, so she is the least threat at that moment and could be guarded loosely, or not at all.

When we had the "extra man" though, the idea was to pass around the circle as quickly as we could to get to our unguarded player. To get there before the defense could adjust, we practiced skipping the nearest player and passing directly to the second or even third (risky…over a lot of defenders' sticks, all raised high) player on the circle, reaching our unguarded player with just two crisp passes.

CLEARING: Clear the ball from the goal we're defending into our attack zone.

The importance of clearing the ball is most evident when your team can't clear. If you can't clear, the other team will eventually score every time they get the ball into their attacking zone. Clearing is mainly the responsibility of the goalie and one or two key players on defense who can run, dodge, and pass their way down the field. Whenever a team has trouble clearing, the other team senses the problem quickly and, like sharks swarming in the water, doubles down and double teams the goalie, marks up tighter on likely receivers and gets even better at stopping the clear.

Midfielders and even those way down the field on attack can aid in clearing. More than once this past season, when we were having difficulties, we had our attack line up close to the restraining line and had the defense or goalie heave the ball over their heads; with luck and practice, our attackers got to the ball first. You can only pull off a stunt like this two or three times in a game.

So that's how we began to build the team at the season's start. Midfield of Amelia, Kendall, and Ayla at the draw (with Claire swapping thereafter). On attack, Lila, Ayla, Ainsley, and Sylvie. On defense, Grace, Zoe, Emma, and…Julia (or Caroline or Flea); and Cali in the goal.

The team that is best in all five functions on a given day will certainly win the game. The team that is best in any three of the five functions will likely win. With so few players during the 2024 season, if a starting player missed a practice or worse, a game, we would do our best to adapt, but this was never easy. We often felt handicapped in such instances as some players had to rethink their roles with little notice.

Chapter 3
The Trouble With Youth Lacrosse Programs

Don't get me wrong. Youth programs for lacrosse, both boys and girls, are prerequisites for a good high school varsity program. High school varsities would not be the same without the youth programs feeding them with enthusiastic, experienced, and sometimes gifted players. The problem is, in youth programs, the fundamentals are too often short-changed. Players develop on their own and can get away with bad habits, probably in part because the pace of the game is much slower than at the high school level. Passes are slower and softer, proper form is not necessary at the youth level and may not be taught, catching can be compromised, goals can be missed, bad passes are overlooked, and missed ground balls are too often forgiven.

I could usually tell if a girl had started playing lacrosse in the third grade or thereabouts; these players typically had little, if any, difficulty with the issues reviewed in this chapter.

It's also a social matter. Younger players may feel self-conscious by, say, crouching into an athletic position until they have become more comfortable as a member of the varsity team.

The fact is, players can graduate from the youth program into high school and bring bad habits with them, habits which, if not identified, worked on, and corrected, can persist and detract from their performance for whole seasons. When freshmen arrive on the scene for the first days of their first high school season, that's the time to introduce remedial work where necessary. In our case for the 2024 season, with nine players new to high school lacrosse, we had four or five who needed remedial work. Since we only had six returning veterans, this was also our only hope for fielding a team of 12 players who could pass and catch under pressure. Here are some of the reasons why remedial training was necessary:

They don't pass correctly. They were never taught to pass by deriving power from their foot on the strong side. That's probably because they didn't need the power in the youth league, and therefore were never taught to pass correctly. Suddenly, they need to make harder, crisper passes in high school. If a player is right-handed, she should pass with her left foot out in front, more or less aimed at the receiver. She should lean back on the right foot slightly, and when she passes, push off with the right foot. This should be a coordinated motion whereby the ball in the stick gets more leverage by incorporating the right foot into the pass. The extra power provided by her right foot will increase the speed of her shot or pass by 50%. I think accuracy improves, as well.

If the player is right-handed and has her right foot extended out in front, the pass is deprived of a lot of potential power and speed. The girl can only pass with her arms. She's likely to just push the ball, with a jerk at the top when she releases the ball, with little or no follow-through. When she uses her right leg to push off, however, bends her knees slightly and leans into the pass or shot, this action becomes a smooth, effective multiplier.

It can take a few days, or possibly a week or so, to change this habit. It will feel awkward at first and require practice, but it will pay off during the rest of the players' high school playing career. It can

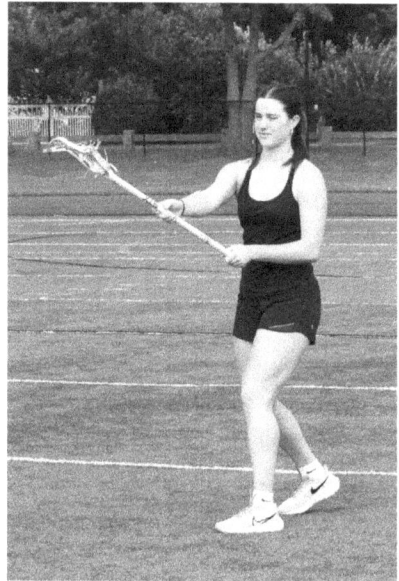

be the difference between being a substitute on the bench versus being a starting player. If left to their own devices during warmup drills, two girls who most need corrective action often wind up having a catch with each other. Neither will learn anything. The girls who need remedial instruction should be paired with the more experienced players who can help them.

They don't catch correctly. Again, this habit is derived from the relatively slower, weaker passes of the youth program. The players catch the ball out in front, they meet the ball head-on and cradle into the ball. Instead, they should meet the ball when it is just slightly in front of their head, and then "give" with the ball, bringing the stick instantly back into a passing position. A good catch can be practiced as the exact reverse motion of a good pass. One of the best drills between two players is to "quick stick" between themselves whereby they catch and pass in one fluid motion, bending at the knees

Here Kendall is bending her knees to compensate for a pass that is coming at her, lower than ideal.

as appropriate. The faster and more accurate the pass, the better.

They don't cradle correctly. There are two ways to cradle correctly. The first is to move both hands in unison, making a smooth curve of the cradle keeping the ball in the same position via centrifugal force. This is fairly easy for most players. The second and more important way is to cradle with the strong hand doing virtually all of the work. The stick is nearly vertical. I teach this cradle by asking the player to "glue" her left thumb to her left thigh, and just use the left hand as a bearing, letting the right hand do all the work, creating all of the centrifugal force to keep the ball in the same position in her stick. Here Kendall is cradling using her right hand but keeping her left hand thumb tight against her thigh. Coaches can help a player get the proper feel of this cradle by taking hold of the very end of the head of the player's stick, and reproducing the cradling motion while the player keeps her right hand loosely holding the stick, enough to get a feel for the proper action, only providing a bearing with her left hand, thumb glued to her thigh.

Kendall cradling using her right hand but keeping her left hand thumb tight against her thigh.

The cradle should be executed with sufficient vigor to resist an opponent's check on her stick without losing the ball. Cradling in the right way is crucial for effective dodging.

They don't scoop up ground balls correctly. This may apply to almost all players at certain times. They can get lazy by not getting low enough, scooping the ball with a stick at a 45-degree angle with the ground. They may get some balls with this approach, but they will not win a competitive ground ball under pressure unless they get low and scoop through

Photo to the left: Wrong. Photo to the right: Better.

on every ball. Players should discipline themselves to always assume an athletic position, bend a little, get low, and scoop through on every ground ball; otherwise, they are not as likely to do it properly under pressure in a game. Games at the level of small and medium schools may be won or lost on the basis of ground balls. At the higher level of play, there are fewer ground balls to begin with, but when they occur, the more advanced players are ready with an athletic stance, bending low, and scooping through.

They don't shoot correctly. This bad habit may also creep into the lexicon of more experienced players. They face the goal instead of turning their bodies away from it, they wind up and shoot, bringing their left hand down on the left side of their body. The ball will invariably go low and to the left of the goal. This happens in early-season games all the time. Under pressure, they forget, face the goal, and shoot bringing their left hand down on their left side and the shot goes low and to the left of the goal. In the first game of each season, I find myself saying, "Aaaagh…the shot to the left of the goal problem," and I start counting the number of shots at the goal that go low and to the left, a number I will bring up for remedial work at our next practice.

I think she's got it.

Of course, it's possible to correct for this by having the shooter pretend the goal is just six feet to the right, she aims at the imaginary goal, and that shot will go right at the goal.

Better yet, what the player should do is turn her body a bit more to the right, clockwise, away from the goal. Then, holding the stick with both hands extended a

Gretchen Kawecki (played for Old Saybrook in 2022 and 2023, Player-of-the-Year as a sophomore) was as close to being ambidextrous as one can be. Though her naturally strong side was right, when passing with her left hand, her right foot goes forward naturally as she derives maximum power from her left foot.

Julia has just taken a shot. She is demonstrating what happens when her left hand comes down on her left side. This shot will invariably go low, missing the goal by going too far to the left. For Julia's next shot (not shown), she will turn her body slightly to her right, bring her left hand down on the right side of her body, and the ball is more likely to hit the goal.

few inches out in front of her, she should shoot, bringing her left hand down on the right side (really, across her midsection) of her body at the end of the shot. The stick moves in a fixed vertical plane relative to the goal, so the ball is at least going to go in the direction of the goal.

We devote 15–20 minutes in many practices to "Time and Room" shots from the 8-meter arc. The players have plenty of time and plenty of room, to shoot as hard and as fast as they can, directing the ball to a specific target in the goal, like the upper right-hand corner (i.e., over the goalie's left shoulder). This is good practice for the penalty shot from the 8-meter arc where, from the instant of the whistle, they have a little bit of time and a little bit of room in which to shoot.

These basics are incredibly important for a small lacrosse team that hopes to fare well during the season, or for any younger player who wants to play lacrosse through high school. These are basics that anyone can practice at home…if the player has a good wall…or a bounce-back… or a friend or sibling to play with.

On our 2024 team, we had 4 or 5 players that could use such improvement. We practiced these moves every day in shuttles…sometimes taking individual players out to explain how to do this or that.

Of course, any high school lacrosse program would be well-served if the youth league in their district taught ten-year-olds how to pass, catch, cradle, shoot, and scoop up ground balls properly.

Here are some photos of Kendall and Julia posing to make certain selected points. Joe Maselli, Julia's father, took the time to set up and take these shots; Kendall and Julia also volunteered their time for this task.

1. The "time and room" shot

Kendall demos her "Time and Room" shot…good for free position "penalty" shots. With her stick so far out in front, there is really no visible distinction between the position of her left hand, whether it's going to

her left or right side…It is definitely not going to her left side though, so this shot will hit the goal.

2. The "run-in on a penalty" shot

Julia demonstrates how to run toward the goal on a free-position penalty shot. Being right-handed, and not having confidence in the long shot from the 8-meter arc, her best options are to pass off to a teammate in a better position to score, hang onto it and resume play, or run for the goal to score closer in. Most in this situation will choose the latter, as Julia demonstrates. Her biggest concern is the defender coming in on the whistle from the hash mark five yards to her right. Ignoring the defender to her left as her stick will always be protected from that side,

Starting on the whistle
at the 8-meter arc.

Start of face dodge before
defender on her right.

Selling her fake to the left.

Quick jig to the right.

Cradles once.

In close enough to shoot.

she face-dodges the defender to her right, jigs to her left briefly, then spurts out to her right, now almost on the crease, and shoots…generally lower right or in the upper right-hand corner.

3. The side arm shot

This shot is not for everyone. In the boy's game, this is standard as their pockets are allowed to go much deeper, and the ball is easier to control than it is with the shallow pockets required for girls. Kendall had a great side arm shot, no doubt derived from her slap shot in ice hockey. This shot was so lethal that, if it was high, i.e., anywhere near the goalie's helmet, referees were inclined to call a "dangerous propelling" penalty on her, with the ominous yellow card (A player receiving two yellow cards is ejected from the game). Kendall used this shot judiciously, especially on lower shots.

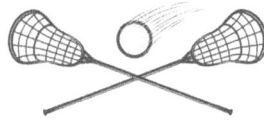

Chapter 4
Practice Plans and Practices

1. The practice plan

It's a good idea for the head coach to prepare a practice plan in writing for each practice. If the head coach is the only coach, it can be hand-written on the back of a 3x5 card. It should spell out the sequence of events and include special notes as reminders of points to cover. In time, I grew to believe in a more detailed, complete practice plan, entered into a computer and printed out to share with other coaches and, when warranted, with captains before the practice sessions. It was also a checklist for me so as not to forget some important aspect.

After most practices, my assistant coach (my son, Rich) and I reviewed the session and discussed how it had gone. The plan versus actual was always part of our evaluation. We were satisfied with about half of our practices; with regard to the other half, we felt we could have done better in some respect.

The practice plan is an important part of the dialogue between the coach and the team. At the end of the season, our players are asked to rate their coach. One of the questions: "Did your coach come to practice prepared?" With a written practice plan at each practice, their answer is more likely to be positive. It's not just for cosmetics, though. Being prepared with a written plan conveys a tone of seriousness to the practice, and is helpful in gaining the team's commitment and enthusiasm for the session. On occasion, the players could suggest a substantive improvement to the plan.

During our regular season in 2024, we had 32 practices. For each one, we had a written practice plan. It pays to spend a few minutes thinking about the next practice beforehand. We tried to articulate a point of emphasis for each practice based on perceived shortcomings from, say, the most recent game. For example: "Point to emphasize today: We will score more points by creating more short passes/feeds to the crease." Or: "Point to emphasize today: Against our next opponent, our clears are more likely to succeed if defenders scatter instantly so the goalie can get off her first clearing pass as quickly as possible." Ideally, we would have a drill for the point to be emphasized, and then incorporate the point into our scrimmage.

Sometimes I shared the plan with other coaches for their comments or to facilitate better preparation. Infrequently, I shared the plan with the captains when I thought they would spend time on it and could add value.

There are many templates for practice plans available on the internet (search: "template for women's lacrosse practice plans"). I used one of these templates when we had three coaches and 35 players at the Coast Guard Academy; at the high school level, though, with just 15 players, it was mostly free-form, as shown below.

This practice was our 8th practice of the season before we had any outside scrimmage or game.

Figure 2: Practice 08, March 26 2024

AREAS OF CONCENTRATION
A. DEFENSE TO PRACTICE RUNNING ALONG SIDELINE (Ayla and Amelia)
1. Conditioning... captain's run, stretches.
2. Shuttles...RHS [Coach] to work with Kendall on sidearm shot.
3. Drills: [note: drills are explained in some detail later in this chapter]
   Box Drill: 4-player box, 3 inside .... Four must pass crisply to "obvious"

teammate. Switch by putting all defense on the corners, defense learns to pass crisply through opponents riding the clear; offense learns to block clearing passes.

4. CLEARING RUNS DOWN THE SIDELINE
5. Brief scrimmage. Handicap: Offense can only score on an assist.
6. End...discussion

Figure 3: Practice 10, April 1 2024

Emphasis Today:
    How to run a fast break
    Defending against a fast break
    Accurate shots under pressure
    Clearing, from goalie to Grace and/or the long pass

Conditioning:
Shuttles: RHS [coach] with all at first, then 1 v 1 with Zoe, Julia, Emma, Caroline

Box drill: offense in corners...alternate. Goalie warm-up

Fast break drill:...Work on at least one pass, better two passes, no more than three before shooting.

Elimination drill: All players on attack, no goalie. Two behind, right and left. Line up to left of center, about 5 yards farther away from goal than the 12-meter. A runs toward 8, fakes left at 10m, veers right and heads for the crease for feed, must shoot at or just beyond the center line. If the play fails because of a shooter error, that shooter is eliminated.

Clearing (Indian circle)...Do 5-6 clears normally; then several clears with the long pass from either goalie or Grace to Ayla or Ainsley on attack behind the restraining line. Ayla is right-handed, so she stands with Ainsley to her right as Ainsley is left-handed. At the moment the goalie or Grace is about to pass, Ayla and Ainsley run toward each other, crossing at the field's center line, a moving pick on their opponents as they each prepare for the long pass on their strong side; goalie or Grace decides which player has the better chance.

Settled offense...how fast can we pass the ball around? No opposition at first, then with opposition

Handicapped scrimmage: score on assists only. Clear after every save.

2. The meeting at the start of practice

If the weather was cold and windy, this is no time for sitting around and talking; on such days, we would move right into a jog around the field before warm-up exercises. On pleasant days, we would start with a discussion of the last game, or the plans for practice this day. Attendance was always the first order of business, as this could dictate some aspects of the practice. For missing players, someone always knew if they were just late, or if they had been missing from school that day (We three coaches were all outsiders, none of us teaching or working within the school, so we had no information in advance on absences). We would also discuss a forthcoming game, key players on the other team, and any intelligence on how they were doing. Then we would start the jog and our "dynamic warm-up."

3. The warm-up

A key purpose of warm-ups is injury prevention, so the more dynamic the warm-up, the better. Start with a run around at least half a field to get the blood flowing to the key joints...hips, knees, and ankles. Our players had their warm-up routines from previous years and from other sports. In addition, we added a few things. For example, we emphasized getting low on lunges and doing side straddle hops. Lots of joint action. [See the chapter on "Injuries"]

4. Shuttles

I was once asked how coaching had changed during the 82 years since my first season as a player (spring of 1942) and my last season as a coach (Spring of 2024). I think it has changed hardly at all from a pure coaching standpoint. Shuttles are a good example. The game changed in remarkable ways, though, as hand-made wooden sticks made by Indian tribes in Canada and upstate New York gave way to plastic or metal sticks and plastic heads mass-produced in factories. Equipment improved greatly (I think of the flimsy upper arm pads tied to shoulder pads using shoe strings). Some rules changed. Title IX led to girls' and women's teams, and the sport became rather ubiquitous throughout the US along with several other countries, mostly in Europe.

I would be surprised to learn that any team anywhere started a practice or game without running shuttles. Just passing the ball back and forth while running toward each other. Then varying it with ground balls, pop-up passes, then passing to the second in line who throws an over-the-shoulder pass to the first in line, etc etc. Shuttles are mostly pure fun. But players can get sloppy, start throwing bad passes resulting in dropped catches, and lost time. Sometimes it's necessary for a coach to count aloud the number of successful passes in a row to restore concentration and focus.

Shuttles are a good time to work on players' weaknesses. Almost all players are dominant right-handed, for example. Some can learn to cradle, pass, and catch with their weak hand, maybe even learn to get off a decent shot. If so, it's a good thing. Very few can play ambidexterously, but if they are also good players, the sky can be the limit for them. We only asked girls to try their weak side. If they could make it work, fine, but it was never a requirement with us.

It is a natural tendency for younger, less experienced players to gather in the same group, leaving the older and more experienced players to do shuttles in their own group. This may seem to make sense as the younger group will drop balls more often, thus causing delays and mild frustration. On the other hand, if you put a junior player in with the older players, the junior player is more likely to learn quickly and play up to the level of her older mentors.

In our practice plans, while most of the team is engaged in shuttles, this is a good time for a coach and/or senior player to warm up the goalie(s).

5. Drills

Any lacrosse coach today is likely to receive, unsolicited, a lot of drills on the internet, especially videos with mostly big-name coaches throughout the country doing the narrating. I generally watched these to see if I could find a kernel of value. These videos were almost all about men's lacrosse, but no matter, they could still be useful and adapted for girls' lacrosse.

At the start of the season, there might be a new player, a freshman, with a drill that she was particularly fond of and wanted to share, or a more seasoned player who had learned of an interesting drill in off-season lacrosse. I usually went along with these offers, with some trepidation lest the drill be a flop, which was often the case. When this happened, we either dropped it or figured out how to make it work. We were always eager to find a new drill to replace one that the team had grown tired of.

There are so many drills, even books of drills; the internet is full of them. Each drill has its pros and cons. Each team should develop its own favorites. During the season of 2024, we zeroed in on a few drills that we could use consistently, that were good for both offensive and defensive skills, that the girls never seemed to tire of, and that best represented live game conditions. Below are five of our favorite drills.

DRILL #1: The Box Drill. This drill is performed with four offensive players forming a box about ten yards square; these players must pass quickly and *crisply* to the "most obvious" teammate on the corners of the square. Inside the square are three defensive players, each eager to block or intercept a pass going from one offensive corner to another. Passes can go left or right, or over the center. I can't explain why this drill worked so well for us, but it did. All players remain focused and competitive.

Offensive players get to fine-tune their passes for live combat. Defensive players learn to hold their sticks high and to slide and slide until it's second nature.

Some caveats with this drill. Offensive players on the corners cannot move off the corner; they must try to keep one foot on the corner. Their passes must be fairly hard, even over the top to a diagonal corner, and they must get rid of the ball quickly to take advantage of the "extra man." Defensive players must slide to another corner (player) with almost every pass. The ten yards between corners was our best measure, but this could be increased for less experienced players.

It's a lively drill that fully engages each player. Substitutions work into this easily. It's a near-game experience. Passers learn to "thread the needle" with their passes. Defenders get the thrill of a blocked or intercepted pass. Our girls rarely tired of this drill before we moved on to something else.

If only they could maintain those crisp and accurate passes in an actual game.

Drill #2: Elimination Drill: Pass, Run, Catch Feed on Crease, and Shoot. This drill evolved over several seasons. In its final form, the coach sends two competent offensive players behind the goal. One on the left and the other on the right. Goalies may be assigned to the goal or not (whenever we put a goalie in the goal for a drill, with no defenders, it was voluntary on the part of the goalie to remain in the goal). The remaining players, the "Shooters," form a line with the bucket of balls about five yards shy of the left-hand corner of the 8-meter arc.

Shooter begins the play by passing to the girl behind left. "Behind Left" passes immediately to "Behind Right" who prepares for a quick feed. Meanwhile, Shooter runs to a spot on the 8-meter arc, jigs to the left, then takes off for a feed from "Behind Right." Her arrival at a good shooting place on the crease is timed to receive the feed from "Behind Right" on her strong side without slowing down.

As soon as Shooter 1 has either shot or missed, Shooter 2 starts the routine again. One trick to this drill is to see how many shooters in a row can get a decent feed and fire off a good shot. The drill goes quickly so there is no time for chit-chat or other diversions. We often used this drill with eliminations rather effectively. If the Shooter causes a broken play or misses the goal, that Shooter drops out. The drill eventually winds down to the two or three best stick handlers on the team that day making rapid-fire passes, getting good feeds, and firing off hard shots into one of the four corners. Cheers for the last Shooter standing.

This drill also works well without eliminations.

Even without defenders (in our case, the defense usually participated in this drill as shooters), this drill has a degree of realistic game aspects.

Drill #3: Out of Chaos, A Disciplined Clear. Defense and offense should wear contrasting pinnies for this drill. The drill is seven v seven. Goalie is in the goal. The fourteen field players gather in a jumble in a circle in the center of the 8-meter arc. They make some sort of chant as they move around in a circle, ensuring a complete mix of players in no particular position relative to one another. The coach tosses the ball to the goalie who yells "CLEAR." The defenders then break for their positions to receive clearing passes, the offense tries to cover the defenders as best they can without regard to who might be assigned to whom. One or two on offense may go to harass the goalie.

This drill gives the defenders a good sense of their positions on a clear. We generally asked two top defensive players to head for the rear-most corners of the field just slightly behind the goal-line-extended (GLE), for a quick pass from the goalie. Other defenders and defensive middies head for the sidelines, spaced well apart from one another so no single member of the other team can guard two defensive players.

This drill also helps the offensive unit practice riding the clear. How quickly can they size up the defensive positions and cover as many players as they can? If they leave the goalie alone, they can play man-to-man and cover the entire defensive unit, eventually compelling the goalie to come out of the goal and proceed down-field, leaving the goal unguarded.

We kept the clearing team away from the middle of the field in practice since a faulty pass intercepted in the middle of the field usually gives the interceptor a pretty good shot at the goal. In actual games, however, by leaving the middle of the field clear, a goalie's pass to a single teammate cutting all by herself through the middle, dangerous as it may be, was often the best path for a clear (again, this worked in our league).

Drill #4: 3 v 2 Fast Break. This is one of the most basic drills of all. We generally started this drill with three offensive players well out in front, coming down toward the goal from midfield. Goalie in the goal. Two defenders come from behind the goal to stop the offense, with the lead defender shouting, "I've got ball." The second defender lags behind, waiting to see which way to slide to intercept the other offensive player most likely to get the next pass. She is hollering to her teammate on the ball, "I've got your back," thus telegraphing to her teammate her location behind her.

On a fast break, the offense has the advantage of an extra man, but only for an instant…the coach's whistle would end any play that dragged on too long. Typically, this play involves two quick, crisp passes and a feed to an open teammate on the crease. Solo dodges were okay…but were generally discouraged in favor of the quick pass or two of team play. The goalie was encouraged to leave the goal to block or intercept any errant feeds.

We used this drill before every game.

Drill #5: Free Position Penalty Shots. We also used this drill before every game. If the other team has fouled one of our players, we may have lost a goal because of it; here is our chance to recover.

Offensive players take a position on one of the hash marks on the 8-meter arc, ready to score on the whistle. The shooter has three options: first, to shoot a "Time and Room" shot from the 8 meter; second, to dodge in through defenders for a close-in shot; or third, to pass to a teammate, usually a surprise to the opponents, which teammate may or may not have a better shot, or who simply takes the ball out to resume settled offensive play. This latter option is especially useful for a shooter who does not feel she can score on this play.

The Time and Room shot from the 8-meter arc is for those players who have a powerful and accurate Time and Room shot. They can hit the goal with a bounce shot, or some can haul off and aim for a corner in the air.

Most players will opt for the dodge and run for the close-in shot. This usually entails a face dodge to bring the stick down and out in front, away from the defender's sticks, a quick jig to her left, and then a dart to the strong side for a short shot, usually high.

The advantage of the third option, the pass-off, can often result in a quick goal by a teammate who happens to be in a good position to receive a feed and shoot. Otherwise, the shooter can simply retain the ball, step back a few paces, and resume the settled offense.

It is important to practice these situations because games can be won or lost by who gets the most penalty shots, and certain players enjoy a high percentage of success on the penalty shots.

6. Scrimmaging

We ended most practices with a scrimmage, generally for about a half hour. (Note: Our school had one turf field; in the spring, half of it was for boys' lacrosse, and the other half for girls' lacrosse. Thus, we only had a half field for scrimmages to begin with). Typically, this would mean a 7 v 7 settled offense. Of course, since we only had 13 players (other than goalies) in 2024, this meant we scrimmaged with 6 v 6, or with an extra man, 7 v 6.

I sometimes found it hard to motivate the defense to take a scrimmage seriously. To counter a natural tendency to slough off, we counted a broken play, or a goalie's save, as a point for the defense. Making a contest out of the scrimmage helped.

Also, we often had a specific goal for the scrimmage that we wanted the offense to take seriously. To accomplish this, we handicapped the offense. "For the next few plays offense can only score on a feed to a teammate, no solo scores."

We could make this more complex. "The offense can only score on a feed to the second cutter."

At practices during the 2024 season, we learned to call the field play from the sidelines, with the coach's command preceding the act by a split second, so the player knew if she should pass, challenge, feed, or shoot. We started with the offense in a settled offense passing the ball around rapidly. The coach (me) is telling each player, loudly, just before she receives the ball, what she should do next. COACH: "Pass, pass, pass, challenge, feed, shoot." This worked so well I kicked myself for not learning this trick years earlier.

7. Wrap-up

We always got together ("bring it in") at the end of a practice and went around the group for comments from captains, coaches, or any other player. Was it a productive practice? Were we ready for the game the next day? What else should we work on at our next practice? Our practices lasted one and a half to two hours. It had to feel like time was well spent. I always hoped the players felt like they had had a good workout…that they had learned something…that they had had a positive experience…and that they were pumped up for the next game.

Chapter 5
Goalies are Special People

The position of goalie in lacrosse, or probably in any contact sport such as ice hockey or soccer, is totally unique. The girl who winds up as goalie by default, e.g., "Let's see a show of hands for those who would like to try out for goalie?" is not likely to be as good as one who volunteers for the position. A good goalie is to be treasured.

Learn Not To Duck

Make no mistake. The balls are hard, and girls can throw a ball almost as hard as boys. With the shallower pockets on girls' sticks, they can't get the leverage that boys can. Nonetheless, a shot from a girl can be plenty fast, causing a girl trying out for goalie to duck. To me, this is the acid test. If a goalie ducks to avoid being hit in the head, she is not a good candidate to be goalie. A girl who is serious about becoming a good goalie can learn not to duck. A coach can train the goalie with slow shots at first, building up to shots as hard as she will encounter in competition. A goalie can't flinch or blink.

I generally warmed up goalies with slow, easy shots to start with, placing the shots all around the goal.

One can shoot at a goalie using tennis balls. I never did.

Coaches may insist that they warm up goalies. I did not.

Or coaches may let the goalie choose who warms them up.

If our goalie is not pumped up for a game, we will lose.

If I warmed up our goalie, I would start just inside the 8-meter arc just passing back and forth with her inside the goal. Next, I threw harder passes (still not at shot speed) to each of nine imaginary locations in the goal…three at the top (left, middle, right), three in the middle and three at the bottom. If she missed any, I repeated that shot. Gradually I increased the speed of the shots and began bouncing a few shots, going from one side to the other. I would move to different angles around the goal, looking for weaknesses, and zeroing in and repeating shots to a weak point. Finally, I would come right up to the crease and shoot at close range just slow enough so she had a chance to stop the ball.

We tried to teach our goalies to bait the shooter. She would deliberately leave a large piece of white net visible to the shooter, virtually begging the shooter to aim for that space. If the shooter took the bait, the goalie was prepared to get her stick quickly into that space.

At most practices, we worked with goalies on the long clearing pass up-field. Devoutly to be wished is the goalie who can make an accurate, long pass up-field to a teammate on attack. We practiced this clear during scrimmages with two *designated* members of the attack close to the restraining line.

Chapter 6
The Shoreline League

The Shoreline Girls' High School Lacrosse League in Connecticut is comprised of seven schools:

- Cromwell
- Haddam-Killingworth (H–K)
- Morgan (Clinton Township)
- North Branford
- Old Lyme
- Old Saybrook
- Valley Regional (serving the towns of Essex, Ivoryton, and Deep River)

During the period from 2018 through 2024, when I was coaching Old Saybrook's team, Old Lyme, North Branford, and Old Saybrook dominated the league, but Morgan, Valley Regional (Essex, Ivoryton and Deep River), and Haddam Killingworth all had respectable seasons during that period. Cromwell's team, though still relatively new and still building, was fast and competitive. You could not take them for granted, ever. We never lost to them but we always had to work hard to win.

During the six playing seasons from 2018 through 2024 (there was no lacrosse season during the COVID era of 2020), four teams had the same head coaches throughout; North Branford, Old Lyme, Morgan, and Old Saybrook. The other three teams, Valley, Cromwell, and H-K, all had coaching changes during that period; this is bound to have an impact on performance.

The existence and quality of youth programs in each of these towns have been an important factor in the performance of each of these teams. The so-called Lyme Ticks, also known as the Connecticut River Lacrosse Club, accepts players from 2nd grade to 8th grade from the towns of Old Lyme, Old Saybrook, Essex, Deep River, Chester, and Ivoryton. I coached in the Ticks program for two years. When I wound up as coach at Old Saybrook, I kept running into players at Old Lyme and Valley Regional (Essex et al) that I had coached when they were with the Ticks. Talk about mixed emotions whenever one of them excelled against us in the high school program.

The Ticks program is serious and well-run, a model for any youth program. Their manifesto below, "Ticks Tough," says a lot.

Figure 4: A Message Before the Season
WHAT IS TICKS TOUGH?

Ticks seeks to create not only a fun and competitive lacrosse environment across our towns, but instill a strong sense of community, sportsmanship, grit, and team first attitude in its players. Leading with the philosophy of "Ticks Tough," we believe firmly that in being a great teammate, respecting coaches, officials, and opponents, and focusing on winning fundamentals we will create long lasting positive outcomes for our players on the field and off. While winning is a goal, our organization is far more interested in the process that goes into it. In registering your player for Ticks, they will not only enhance their passion and learning of lacrosse, but be challenged to be an excellent team-mate, sportsman, and leader.

We encourage all our players, coaches, volunteers to abide by "Ticks Tough." Being Ticks Tough means:

1.) Respect – Player respects coaches, referees, opponents and teammates
2.) 3 E's – Effort, Enthusiasm, Energy on the field and off

3.) Fun – Player is having fun and ensures their teammates are as well
4.) Player Foundations built around:
   - Dominating Groundballs
   - Creating and Seeking Turnovers
   - Stellar Defense
   - Pass then Shoot Mentality
   - Sportsmanship
5.) Ours over Mine, We over Me Mentality

Figure 5: The Original Schedule and Results for the 2024 Season

Date	Opponent	Scrimmage?	Home/ Away	Result...First score Old Saybrook
Wed., 3/27	Montville	Scrimmage	Away	Won 22–14, unofficial
Thu., 3/28	Waterford	Scrimmage	Away	Lost 3–17, game played April 27
Tue., 4/2	**North Branford**		Away	Lost 10 - 11, game played April 29
Thu., 4/4	**Morgan (Clinton)**		Home	Won 12–5
Sat., 4/6	Fitch (Groton)		Home	Lost 2–14
Wed., 4/10	**Old Lyme**		Home	Lost 6–14, game played May 4
Sat., 4/13	New Fairfield		Away	Lost 16–5
Tue., 4/16	**Valley Regional**		Away	Won 20–6
Thu., 4/18	**Haddam Killingworth**		Home	Won 11–7
Tue., 4/23	**Cromwell**		Away	Won 17–4
Fri., 4/26	**Old Lyme**		Away	Lost 6–8
Sat., 4/27	St Bernard		Home	Game not played
Thu., 5/2	**North Branford**		Home	Won 13–9
Tue., 5/7	**Haddam Killingworth**		Away	Won 14–13
Thu., 5/9	**Morgan**		Away	Won 12–8
Sat., 5/11	St Bernard		Away	Game not played
Tue., 5/14	**Cromwell**		Home	Won 16–4
Thu., 5/16	**Valley Regional**		Home	Won 16–7

Teams in **Bold** are in the Shoreline League

Old Saybrook's record in the regular season, Shoreline League, 9–3, losing two games to Old Lyme, one to North Branford (League Champion)

Shoreline Conference Playoffs

	North Branford	Away	Lost 8–10
5/24–25 First Round States			
	Wheeler	Home	Lost 13–15

Chapter 7
Basic Principles, Protocols, and Guidelines

*"A coach is someone who can
give correction without resentment."*
—*John Wooden*

Lacrosse may be the oldest competitive team sport the world has seen. In the National Museum of the American Indian in Washington, DC, there is a lacrosse stick from Indigenous tribes that is 2,000 years old. For the rest of the world, however, the sport essentially began at the start of the 20th Century. In those early days, the sport existed only in a few high school enclaves in the US, especially in schools on Long Island, New York, in schools in and around Baltimore, and in private schools in New England. Sticks were made of wood, crafted by Indigenous tribes in the Eastern US and Canada; this limited the growth of a sport as popular as lacrosse until plastic sticks were mass-produced in the 1970s. The passage of Title IX about that same time, in 1972, had a huge impact on girls' and women's lacrosse. Today, lacrosse is played nationwide, is still growing rapidly, and has, as the lead institution for the sport in the United States, US Lacrosse. The sport evolved with certain traditions, some of which are observed throughout the lacrosse world today.

Never play favorites. I truly believe (Actually, I really know this) that every player on my team is equally important…perhaps not to the team as a player, but to all of us as persons. This applies to the star as well as the struggling newcomer. I might spend more time with some players than others, but I always tried to spend some time with each player. This is tough if you're the only coach with 35 players, but that is unlikely to happen. We had 35 players at the Coast Guard Academy, but I always had at least one assistant coach to help with such matters. I never cut a player from any of my teams. If you wanted to play lacrosse on my team, you were welcome. I can envision situations where this is not practical, but I was never in such a situation. If I haven't personally communicated with a player for a while, I pull her out of the shuttle and have a catch with her, something like that, and try to give her a pointer to improve her passing or catching. "If you would just bend your knees and lean back on your right foot a little before you pass…"

In the warmups before a game, I try to have a brief one-on-one catch with every player starting in the game. Passes as hard and as accurate as the two of us can handle. If I can think of one, I like to have an encouraging or aspirational comment to make to each of them.

Some of these young people struggle with things at home that are invisible to those of us on the lacrosse field. Lacrosse can be an important social connection. I can't see it, but I know it's there and must be respected. Social cliques are to be avoided, and for managing this, we relied heavily on our captains. Once in the women's game, I encountered a serious case of bullying. A few teammates had it in for another. It was so egregious and concealed that ever since I have kept a watchful eye out for any signs or circumstances that might indicate bullying. If any player ever says something bad to the coach about another player, assume it's not true…because it's not…but make note of who said it.

When the whistle blows to start a lacrosse game, the minds of every player and coach must be focused totally on the events of the moment. At such times, no serious player can be thinking about her problems at home or school or elsewhere. Lacrosse is a release from everything else, consuming its participants for the next hour.

No standing around. I remember high school drills when I was a player that could be dreadfully dull. Over-the-shoulder clearing passes, for example. Long lines as you waited your turn. Boys can generally suffer through this…girls can't. If we create a drill with long wait times, pretty soon the players begin to chatter about things besides lacrosse and take their mind off the game. Whenever we would try a new drill, if it's not going well, we quickly scrapped it and moved on to something that's tried and true. We constantly revised drills to reduce waiting times, and to maintain interest and focus.

Playing time for substitutes. It was a good experience to have coached at both public and private schools; there are differences. Take playing time. Parents of students in private schools are much more likely to complain that their daughter is not getting enough playing time. After all, that's part of what they pay extra for. But more playing time for some may mean lowering the chances of winning for the rest of the team. We tried to create reasonable expectations. Let every player know what she can expect when it comes to playing time. A second-string goalie has to know that her chances of getting in an important game may be close to zero, for example. If that's the case, we make sure she knows in advance.

The best answer for playing times in our case this past season were games where our team had a decided advantage. Our three junior players, Julia, Caroline, and Flea, each had plenty of playing time in several such games this season even though they may have played relatively little in the more important games. Our second-string goalie, Erin, also had ample opportunities to prove her mettle.

I received one email from a mother in 2024 who felt we had mistreated her daughter. She was right. We had. We had started her daughter, ordinarily a substitute, in one game due to the absence of other players. Her name thus remained by accident on our roster in the scorebook as a starter for the next game, in which she would not start. It was a game for which there would be loudspeakers to announce each of the players as they ran out onto the field. This girl was announced as a starting player when she wasn't. We even had her jersey number wrong. All our fault. We tried to make it up to her in subsequent games. One can never afford to become complacent about such matters. We might inadvertently commit other slights from time to time, but it was up to the coaches as a group, sometimes with input from captains, to be sensitive to such things.

Of course, playing time is a moot point when there are enough players to field a junior varsity. In our league, that number was around a minimum of 18 players. Our league cheerfully played JV games with fewer players, like 7 v 7, or even 6 v 6 to accommodate rivals with fewer players. It was usually easy to persuade at least one varsity player to play in the JV game. If we had 18 or more players, we would have at least 6 who wouldn't start in the varsity game. Because of the way I coached our small teams by relying on the starting 12 to play an entire game, these 6 might get very little playing time in a close game; but they might play for the entire JV game and have a rip-roaring time of it. No complaints from the players or their parents. In the spring of 2024, with just 15 players, one of whom was including a substitute goalie, we had no chance to field a JV team.

Control of lopsided scores. How does one control against running up a score? I've been accused of such, but we never deliberately let our team run up a score. I've been in debates with other coaches who say they tell their star players to stop scoring if they get up to, say, 5 goals. I won't ask a player to play down. It's bad psychology. I do like to see our team settle the ball which is often the right tactic anyway, which slows down the pace of scoring. We did not seek slowdowns because it may be at the expense of a star player out to break some invisible (to me) record, such as a 100th or 200th career goal scored. Who am I to interfere with a girl's chances of getting a big lacrosse scholarship? Number of goals and assists can play a role in such matters. Our rule was, that once we were leading by ten goals, it was time to give the substitutes a chance to play. We controlled against lopsided scores in our favor by substitutions.

A lopsided game can also be good for the better team to develop a certain team skill, like practicing short passes to teammates on the crease. Our teams were only occasionally good at using a lopsided game for such an opportunity, say, to work on some aspect of team play. More likely, we would use such a game as an opportunity for less experienced players. In 2024, with only 2 field substitutes, they saw lots of playing time against teams where we had the upper hand. I know they benefitted from it.

Give credit where credit is due. At the first practice after a game, we always reviewed the game with the whole team. If it was especially deserved, I liked to start with how the defense and goalie did as the defense gets too little credit in general. Or we started with offensive goals and assists. Or we might start with our performance at the draw circle if we had done particularly well, and for which we generally had good stats. Next, I would congratulate the high scorer of the game and work my way down to the last assist. Or, we would reverse the order and start with the player who may have just scored a single assist, and work our way up to the player who had just played her "best game ever." As the scorebook was the official record of the game, if players had a different recollection of who scored or assisted, and how many, this was the time to set the record straight…an important function. I was especially pleased any time our seven starters on offense had all scored or assisted. Those were examples of great teamwork. There was always something good to say about everyone, even an offensive player who hadn't scored or assisted at all. Perhaps she had caused a turnover or had scrambled and gotten a tough ground ball. With regard to defense, we typically had no stats such as forced turnovers. When they could, our scorers recorded the number of successful clears. We could generally recall at least one outstanding play by every player on the field. If one of the substitutes had simply gotten the ball, handled it, and passed off successfully, that could be worth a round of applause. Goalies were recognized by the number of saves, and by the occasional interceptions, or exceptional clearing passes. At the end of these sessions, every player should know that if she did her best, everybody knew and appreciated it.

Coaching from the sidelines. I think some coaches believe it is their obligation to coach from the sidelines…yelling advice to players throughout the game as if they were still on the practice field. In certain professional sports, the coaches are an important part of the act, part of what people pay to see. Not so in lacrosse, at least in my opinion. Get your team ready for the game, and then leave it to them to figure out what to do on the field. From the sidelines, we don't really know what's happening out on the field of combat. That's what captains are for. If a coach has something important to say to a player on the field in mid-game, and it's not a good time to use up a precious time out, we would send in a substitute, telling the sub she was only going to be in for a matter of a few seconds, have the conversation with the player and send her right back in. This can also be especially important if one suspects the player on the field is getting overly emotional about something and may need to come out altogether to regain her composure…in which case, the sub may get more playing time than she had anticipated, not a bad thing.

Complaints about referees. One year, I was 82 at the time, I became a certified referee for girls' lacrosse in Connecticut. The final act of certification was a half day of refereeing four short 20-minute games between 8:00 and 1:00, with veteran referees overseeing everything. The weather that day was windy and cold, with intermittent light rain and occasional snowflakes. I was not in adequate shape for this ordeal. By the time of my fourth game, I was completely done in. When I was finally free to go home, I hauled my aching bones into the car and sat there for an entire hour before I even started the engine. Maybe my wife was right… again…I had bitten off more than I could chew. I refereed a few games, but it was not for me…I went back to coaching in the local youth league. This experience gave me great respect for referees, though. Whenever our players would complain about the refs in a game, my response was, "They make mistakes. Deal with it." In our first game against North Branford in 2024, we lost by one goal. During the game, one shot by a North Branford player bounced off the top bar of the goal and rebounded almost straight down, but off to one side. From the physics alone, the ball could not have passed through the plane of the goal, so it was not a goal; the referee ruled it a goal. They could even make mistakes that cost us a critical game.

There was one ref, however, in our game against non-league Ledyard in 2023, with whom I had a problem. In the opening seconds of the game, a Ledyard player lost the ball and it went out of bounds off of her, right in front of me. The referee gave the ball back to the Ledyard player. It was so flagrant I reacted on impulse and shouted, "Hey Ref, that should be our ball." The referee doubled down. For the remainder of the game, he was abusive to our team, giving us dubious penalties, and siding with Ledyard whenever possible. It was painful. The next year, 2024, he was assigned to our league, and I could feel that the grudge lingered on. I had to tell myself, "Deal with it!"

For any single event that could be blamed on a referee, that team could look to at least two opportunities to score that they blew. The last distraction any team needs is to blame their inadequacies and short-comings on the referees.

Goals and objectives for the season. At the start of each season, we always had a discussion with the team about our goals for the season. Invariably, one player would say, "To win." To win, but at what cost? I can recall games where we won, but afterward, I didn't feel all that good about our win; we had played badly. I have felt good after games we lost if we played well, if we gave it our all, if it was a good game…the other team just happened to be the better of the two on that day. Our goal for 2024 was gently steered by coaches and captains in the direction of, "To be the best we can be when we have to be our best."

We adopted a corollary: "To have fun." I knew this to be true, that girls not only want to play well and win, they also want to have a good time doing it. This was hard for me. I'm not fun. At the age of 90 during the season of 2024, I was fortunate to have two much younger coaches, one, my son, Rich, and the other, a young lady in her early twenties, Emily Haviland, who had played lacrosse herself and had a good way with the girls.

I had some great coaches in sports and in life. From the time I was in the 8th grade until I graduated from high school, my lacrosse coach was Bob Hulburd. Bob had been captain of the Princeton University lacrosse team in 1943. He then joined the Navy and crossed the English Channel 80 times transporting troops into battle in the period following D-Day. He came to my school the same year I did, in the fall of 1946. There was no lacrosse program at this school, but I had already played lacrosse for five years at my previous school in Baltimore. In the fall of 1946, Bob asked if I would like to help him build a lacrosse program at our school. Hulburd was what a great coach should be: he was a good player himself; he really knew the game. He was patient. He was firm. He was well-liked…students wanted to play for him. He was a humanist…"every player is equally important." Without Hulburd, I would not have played lacrosse in high school, college, and clubs and I would never have coached the sport. Bob Hulburd had a big impact on my life. He had all of the qualities that I associate today with Coach John Wooden of NBA fame.

John Wooden analyzed the sport of basketball in excruciating detail, starting at the high school level. He invented his "Pyramid of Success," a pyramid-shaped diagram which, at the bottom has the individual fundamentals essential for success as a team player: Industriousness, friendship, loyalty, cooperation, and enthusiasm. It works its way up to the second level with self-control, alertness, initiative, and intentness. Moving up the pyramid to the third level, we get to specific sports-related issues including conditioning, skills, and team spirit. The last two before reaching the top of the pyramid, competitive greatness, are poise and confidence. One year, I gave each player a copy of this pyramid and asked them to tell me where they thought they were on this pyramid, and where they would like to get to during the coming season. It may have been helpful. Some girls got more out of it than others. I never used the pyramid in that way again, but I have used it with certain players each year who asked for help in improving their team skills, their leadership qualities, or their relationships with other players on the team; sometimes it's helpful to know that others have trod certain paths long before with success, and therefore "you can do it, too." There is also the introspective mindfulness of the Wooden approach; some girls adopted the Wooden approach as their own and employed its use in their everyday lives in addition to sports.

Wooden derived his coaching rules from and for basketball; I believe his constructs are even more applicable to the sport of lacrosse, and to lacrosse players and teams, than they are to basketball. Almost any lacrosse coach could benefit from a study of John Wooden's contribution to coaching in its broadest sense.

Electing captains. Madeline Kawecki played on our team her senior year in 2018. When the team was asked for volunteers to become captain, there were plenty of seniors, and when it was her turn, Madeline declined. She said she didn't want to be captain, but looked forward to helping any player who might seek her help. Madeline turned out to be a great leader and example for our team without being a captain. One doesn't have to be a captain to be a positive influence on a team.

But teams need captains, and we always had at least two, and one time, four. When the captain decisions were up to the coaches and not an athletic director, we voted democratically. Candidates would make a short speech as to why they would like to be captain. Then we passed out ballots and counted them secretly. We deferred to captains on many decisions…especially when to have special practice sessions. We always sought the opinions of captains when, say, due to an injury, we had to make a sudden decision as to who should take her place. What we may have thought was an obvious choice was not always the case.

Taunting and foul language on the field. I never experienced this during the 16 years or so that I played lacrosse. In boys' and men's lacrosse, dirty playing was physical, not verbal ("Hmmm…Was that sharp jab into my kidneys from the butt end of that defenseman's big wooden stick an accident?"); it was also rare. As coach of the Women's team at the Coast Guard Academy, however, we did experience foul, taunting language with one college (my rule was: if one cadet complained about the behavior of an opposing player, I would be dismissive of the matter, "Suck it up"; if a second cadet complained about the same player, however, it was incontrovertible truth and maybe *I* should deal with it). The following year, that college had trouble finding opponents willing to play them. At our level of play in high school, we experienced the occasional verbal taunts from fans, one or two heavily-engaged parents, but only rarely among players on the field. When I heard about such things, I could rely on Lila to tell me exactly what was said. Sometimes what she told me was unprintable when I was growing up… and still is today. I put this in the same category as having a beef with referees: "Deal with it!"

No gloating. There is a proper and an improper way to deal with winning. It's natural to be excited when your team has won, especially a hard-fought contest, and the players can cheer their hearts out. There is a time for celebration immediately after the game is over. There is also a time to cheer when your team executes a brilliant play and scores, or when it breaks up a brilliant play by an opponent. When a player is coming off the field with an injury, however, that is no time to cheer. Or even when a top player gets her second yellow card and must exit the game. That's not a time for the other team to cheer, either. It can be disruptive to a losing team to have their winning opponents cheer in a huddle in the middle of a game for no apparent reason, like when one of their players has just broken a career record. Since no one knows why they are cheering, this can come across as gloating. Coaches have to be sensitive to such situations and guard against appearing to gloat at the other team's expense.

It is the custom in lacrosse, and in many sports today, for each team and coaches to line up after a game ends and shake hands (or fist bump) with each player and coach from the opposing team. While it can come off as perfunctory, it's really an important custom. Win or lose, this is the time for the two teams to show respect for one another, and for the sport. Just because you lost the game and you're upset is no reason to miss this ritual. I think of the player on another team who had counted on a game with us to be her showcase to stardom, but she and her team went down ignominiously. She skipped out on the post-game handshake. It was noticed.

I like to at least shake hands with the opposing coach as soon as practical after a game, win or lose; if the winning coach is off celebrating with his or her team, for 10 or 15 minutes before shaking hands, that feels like rubbing it in.

Goals versus assists. I like to ask our team at the beginning of a season, "Which is more important, the goal or the assist?" It is always an interesting and constructive discussion. In the old days, a player's rank was determined by points, two points for a goal, and one for an assist. That changed somewhere along the line to a system based on one point for each. In other words, the lacrosse establishment determined that the goal and the assist should be counted as equals. But the discussion is always interesting. A goal is personal, announced, and published for all to hear and see, forever, sometimes…and here's the rub…bordering on the selfish. An assist, on the other hand, is also recorded if the scorer saw correctly who made it, but it is much more behind the scenes, quietly crucial but inconspicuous…it is an unselfish act for the team…largely forgotten. The talented player who can make the split-second decision to score or feed based on what is best for the team is a player to be revered and emulated. I've seen many potentially great players work through this thought process and eventually reach the right conclusions, if not in their freshman year, then in the next year or the next.

Life lessons. Sports are full of life lessons. Team sports have a lot. Intense, physically-competitive team sports like football, basketball, field hockey, ice hockey, and lacrosse offer the most life lessons of all. Except for soccer, these latter sports are almost all typically American, at least at the high school level. In most of Europe, sports are the province of private, non-profit clubs, connected to a town or municipality, not connected to any school or college. A club may offer multiple sports, or just one (say, soccer). I believe the American system enriches society as a whole in the best possible way. Title IX, the civil rights legislation of the seventies, banned discrimination on the basis of sex from any educational activity receiving federal funding. While not directed specifically at sports, this legislation affected sports, and opportunities for girls and women, in spectacular ways. Girls' and women's lacrosse benefitted greatly, from greatly improved programs at the high school level to lucrative sports-related scholarships for college. Title IX raised the level of self-confidence among girls and women all over America; it gave them the confidence to plunge into, and succeed, in almost any area of human activity.

The life lessons of lacrosse are abundant. Learn to cope with failure. If you make a mistake, don't dwell on it, get over it quickly and move on. If you work hard enough at something, you will get better, and sooner or later, you will succeed. When your emotions tell you to do one thing, and your brain tells you to do another, go with your brain. Life is never fair. Deal with it. You don't have to do everything yourself; you may accomplish more by relying on or sharing the limelight with others. When things are going your way, that's the very time to be humble. When you're interviewed by the press after winning an important game, compliment the other team, no matter what you may think of them.

Build for the Future. During the season, every player is likely to develop in various ways and in varying degrees. Seniors will have pretty much reached their peak of performance for their last season in high school. Some will be planning to play in college, club if not varsity. Juniors may want letters of recommendation. My letters of recommendation tend to be aspirational, what I believe and hope for this player. When she reads my letter (if that's allowed by the college), she should recognize herself, and be happy with the positive attributes. If they are ever-so-slightly overstated, which would be my inclination, then maybe the letter will prove to be motivational for the player. For the sophomores, and especially the freshmen, of course, they have two or three additional seasons each; they will grow, they will get stronger, they will run faster...and they will improve their stickhandling and field play. If they have a wall or bounce-back at home, there may be some particular aspect to work on, such as passing and catching properly...and a great way just to pass the time. They may have someone else with whom they can have an occasional catch. I find the basic movements associated with time and room shots something players can work on all year long...and enjoy doing it. We show them how. If two freshmen are aspiring members of the attack, we may pull them out of shuttles or regular drills and ask them to work on teamwork between themselves, like feeding and shooting around the crease; the two of them could become a force together by their senior year.

Chapter 8
What It Means to "Win At All Costs"

I hate to lose…but…

- If we lost, and in addition, we played badly, that's the pits.
- If we won but played badly, that's almost as bad.
- If we played well and lost…I'm actually okay with that.
- If we played well and won…especially against a "*better*" team… by a hair's breadth…in the closing seconds…that's sheer joy.

To some coaches, winning is everything. To win at all costs at the high school level can mean:

1. Local referees deliberately penalizing a visiting team to benefit, unfairly, the home team.
2. Players using abusive language to rile an opponent.
3. Fans from one team taunting the opposing team's players by calling them out by name or number, or singling them out by any means for taunts.
4. Bypassing traditions such as the post-game handshake of all players and coaches.
5. Inciting one's players to be overly aggressive in a heated contest, penalties be damned.

6. Player coming off the field because of a major penalty, to muffled applause by her teammates.

While rare, I experienced all of these things while coaching girls' and women's lacrosse. At Old Saybrook, we explained to our players before the first game the kind of behavior that was unacceptable. I think that's all that is necessary.

Chapter 9
Injuries
Preventing and Recovering From Them

On game days, I always put a half dozen band-aids in my pocket. Ninety percent of all lacrosse injuries in girls' lacrosse could be handled with a band-aid, little cuts on the hands and legs that bled enough for a referee to blow a whistle and ask the player to leave the game. The band-aids in my pocket enabled us to patch up minor wounds quickly, during a time-out or even while the clock was running, so we wouldn't have to send in a substitute.

At games, the school's professional trainer was present in case of more serious injuries. Most of the time, the trainer was able to take care of the problem and the girl was able to return to the game. On rare occasions, the player was unable to return to the game. To my recollection, we did not have a player out of the game for more than a few minutes during the 2024 season.

Two injuries concerned me as a coach of girls' lacrosse; torn

Kendall Dobratz with two black eyes from getting whacked on the nose by an opponent.

ACLs and concussions. The former can be prevented to an extent with informed parents and coaches. The latter can be treated in ways that are not yet condoned by the US government.

TORN ACL

In his book, *Warrior Girls: Protecting Our Daughters Against the Epidemic in Women's Sports,* Michael Sokolove goes into great detail in explaining the ACL injury whereby players tear the Anterior Cruciate Ligament (ACL); this is one of the main ligaments that connects the thigh bone or femur to the shinbone, or tibia. When it tears, there is pain and swelling at the knee. Surgery to repair the ACL is often required. Recovery and rehabilitation generally take up to a year, with the athlete missing an entire season.

Sokolove makes the point that for the same athletic effort, girls are 8 times more likely than boys to tear their ACL. Sokolove focuses on soccer, but lacrosse is not far behind. He makes the point that it is good to strengthen the muscles and other tissues around the knees via dynamic warm-up exercises.

At the Williams School where I coached girls' lacrosse, there was a steep hill, maybe 15 feet high at an angle of 30 degrees, between two playing fields. We used this hill in almost every practice. The players would walk up facing forward, then turn around and walk back down… then go up and down facing to one side, then up and down facing the other side…and finally, going up and down backward…etc., etc. As the entire team crunched and ground their way up or down the hill, you could almost hear their sinews getting stronger.

We did sprints in most practices using several variations. First, a straight line for 50 yards, at top speed, without sticks, several times. The fastest players were recognized. On the 2024 team, Ainsley, Lila, Ayla, and Kendall were generally among the fastest. Then the same thing, but cradling with sticks and balls, also several times. Then the same thing cradling with sticks and balls and doing a face-dodge and 360 turn along the way. In the 2024 season, we did the so-called ladder sprints whereby the players would run five yards, turn and run back, then run ten yards and turn back, then 15 yards and run back. The ladder sprints are particularly good for strengthening lower body joints.

We had two players out for an entire year, each because of torn ACLs, one in 2022, and one in 2023. Both were great players, and both were captains. Both had torn their ACLs in off-season lacrosse. I'm not a big fan of off-season lacrosse. For one thing, it seems to me the focus in off-season sports is more on individual play rather than team play; when the high school season rolls around there is some reverse pedaling required to get players back into a team frame of mind.

Secondly, and I've seen this first hand, girls are apt to go into off-season games with too little warm-up time and the ACL is tight. It tears with the extreme effort and stress on joints required when, say, dodging and spinning toward the goal for a score, or twisting and suddenly reversing direction to get a competitive ground ball. Invariably it is your better players who will demand more than their bodies can deliver.

As I have now retired from coaching and no longer need to be superstitious, one thing I could look back on was 13 years of coaching high school girls and college women, over 200 players, more than 200 games and 300 practices, without a single torn or injured ACL. Just lucky?

CONCUSSION

I recall maybe 2 injuries that impacted a player for more than a week; both were boys, and both involved a broken bone. The worst injury I ever experienced as a coach, though, was during my first season at Old Saybrook High School in the spring of 2018.

The captain of the Old Saybrook team that year was Kendall Hartt. Kendall was a seasoned player who understood, better than any other player I ever coached, the meaning of Yogi Berra's iconic expression when it came to center draws or ground balls: "It ain't over till it's over." Kendall had the determination, perseverance, athleticism, and guts to stay in the fracas full bore until she had the ball in her stick and under her control. I could not have anticipated a better captain to work with that year. Kendall was the main reason that we had a successful season and that I was invited to continue as head coach at Old Saybrook.

At one point in a non-league game early in the season, Kendall was suddenly lying on the field out cold. The referees saw nothing. I saw nothing. Kendall recalled nothing. If she was hit by an opposing player, no one saw it happen. But there was Kendall, out cold with a blow to the head. The trainer was on the spot and called 911. The ambulance arrived at the field. Since driving a vehicle across the new track was prohibited, they had to roll a gurney out onto the field. Precious minutes went by. Kendall had been lying on the field for at least 20 minutes. By this time, she had recovered somewhat and was speaking with the medics.

After they wheeled her off the field, I cancelled the game and the JV game to follow. I had no stomach for more lacrosse that afternoon and feared the worst for Kendall. The next day at practice, however, and on the field when I arrived, there was Kendall…looking perfectly fine and smiling. I was stunned. She couldn't play for a few days while her doctor and our trainer guided her through the concussion protocols, but was otherwise unhurt. Kendall went on to play varsity lacrosse at Drew University in Madison, New Jersey, where she starred on, no surprise to me, draws and ground balls.

Kendall was an inspiration. At one point she told me she planned to be an orthodontist; I thought to myself, "There will not be a crooked tooth left in America."

The protocols for recovery from a concussion are explicit, and every lacrosse coach in CT must take a concussion refresher course each year. If a player has had a concussion, the recovery is monitored by a medical doctor. When the doctor clears the player to return to practice, the athlete's recovery and "return to play" decision then falls under the responsibility of the school's trainer. The trainer directs the athlete's "return to play," starting with light practice and no contact at first, moving gradually back to full-contact play. Coaches and parents have no say in this process, and cannot influence the "return to play" decision in any way.

If any athlete suffers a concussion, it is vitally important that the athlete not incur a second concussion before the first concussion heals.

While there is no exercise or conditioning to prevent a concussion, there is one medical treatment that should be considered by parents of players who suspect that there are lingering signs of a concussion in the behavior of their daughter. That treatment is HyperBaric Oxygen Therapy, or HBOT.

HBOT involves placing a patient in a pressure chamber (or room) for a period of time (typically an hour per dive) that simulates diving underwater to a depth of, say, 15 or 30 feet. The extra oxygen helps heal damaged parts of the brain. A prescribed treatment for an injury may involve several or even many "dives" over a period of weeks, dozens or even a hundred or more for a single patient. And each "dive" costs money.

HBOT has been used extensively to cure soldiers wounded by explosives on the battlefield, and suffering from Post Traumatic Stress Disorder (PTSD) or Traumatic Brain Injury (TBI). The problem is, HBOT has not been approved by the National Institute of Health or the Food and Drug Administration (and therefore by the Veterans Administration) as "evidence-based medicine" for treating brain injuries; the hold-up is extremely controversial as the reason may be mainly a matter of money rather than what's best for the patients. More than 300,000 American veterans are suffering from brain injuries; if the average patient needed, say, 100 dives for treatment, at a cost, say, of $100 per dive, that would come to $10,000 per patient; for all 300,000 wounded veterans with brain injuries, the cost would reach $3 billion.

Several thousand wounded veterans have received HBOT treatments, funded privately, with amazingly positive results; the downside, or risks, have been largely negligible compared to the potential benefits. This is not enough, however, to persuade entrenched bureaucrats of the error in their ways; could they be waiting for those 300,000 veterans to die off?

Treatnow.org, a no-profit organization has been keeping track of this process for the past ten years or so. That this treatment is applicable for sports injuries, notably NFL football players, many of whom develop diagnosable brain trouble later in life long after they have retired from football, there is no doubt. While it is best to treat a brain injury sooner rather than later (Treatnow.org has recommended placing HBOT chambers close to American battlefields), treating later, no matter how much later, may still be helpful.

Without belaboring the point further, if I had a daughter, an athlete who had suffered a concussion, been released by her doctor and trainer to return to full contact play, but from whose behavior I sensed that she had never fully recovered from the blow, I would contact Treatnow.org. I would seek their advice about, and hopefully prescribe, the use of HBOT.

As for helmets and girls' lacrosse, helmets are mandatory in Florida, but nowhere else in the US. Any girl can wear a helmet today, but few do. The coach of the Stonington (CT) Girls' Lacrosse Team requires that his players wear the helmet prescribed for girls' lacrosse. One way or another, concussions should and will become less of a problem for female athletes in the future.

Chapter 10
Parents and Athletic Directors

Coaches serve at the pleasure of athletic directors; they also serve with or without the consent of parents. "With" is better.

My first coaching job was coach of the Ohio State University Freshmen Men's team in the spring of 1960. I was finishing up a graduate degree at OSU at the time and wandered out to the lacrosse field one day out of curiosity. The Ohio State Varsity Lacrosse coach hired me as a volunteer to coach the freshman team. I don't recall meeting any parent of any members of this team, nor did I ever meet anyone from the athletic department.

When my son, Rich, and I started the boy's lacrosse program in the Mountain Lakes, NJ, school system in 1974, parents became enthusiastic supporters of a strange sport they knew little about other than that it excited their children. The first year we had 15 players at the middle-school level. In the second year, we had 35 players in three different age groups, high school, middle school, and the very young. Parents provided transportation to games (no Bluebird busses as the sport had not yet been sanctioned by the school system). Parents provided sustenance at games…water, fruit, and sandwiches. They created a photo album of the season. They gave me an embroidered coach's jacket which I still have today. I left Mountain Lakes in 1976 to take a job in a place and situation far away from lacrosse. An All-American lacrosse player from Dartmouth, graduating class of 1962, John Walters, moved into town a few months before I left. When we met and I learned of his background,

I must have said something like, "John, have I got a deal for you." John took on the challenge, integrated the program with the school, saw that funds were budgeted for the program, and supported the school in hiring its first paid lacrosse coach, Tim Flynn. Flynn became one of the most successful high school lacrosse coaches in the country.

A few years ago, we visited Mountain Lakes during the lacrosse season. There was a lacrosse goal in the backyard of every third house in town. Coach Flynn told us that 250 school-age kids in this small town were playing lacrosse, about 50/50 boys to girls, in five different age categories.

When I coached the Victoria Men's Lacrosse Club in Berlin, Germany (2006–2007), I met some parents, but the players were almost all college graduates, taking time off from work to play lacrosse.

The players hired me to be their volunteer coach. That first year the team won the championship of Eastern Germany (now called the Lacrosse League of Northeast Germany). At the time, there were four teams in the league (Dresden, Leipzig, Cottbus, and Berlin); today, just 18 years later, and a testament to the growth potential of lacrosse, there are more than fifty teams in that league. Team Victoria gave me a generously embroidered jacket suitable for evening wear, a jacket I still have today though I have not yet had an occasion to wear it in public.

In the spring of 2008, I applied for and was accepted as assistant coach of the Men's Lacrosse Team at the US Coast Guard Academy. At the last moment, however, I was asked by the advisor to the women's team, Captain Anne Flammang, to be assistant coach of the Women's team, my first encounter with the female version of the game (Now retired, Anne Flammang was a formidable officer who left a legacy of courage and principle while in the Coast Guard). Keith Curran, father of cadet Brittany Curran, was the volunteer head coach; Brittany was a senior and co-captain. Keith had played the game and was in the Coast Guard himself. The following year, Brittany graduated, Keith went off to other pursuits, and I became head coach of this team for the next three years. Many parents came to the weekend games. They did more than tailgate; they had tents and grills, and made an occasion out of away games as well as home games, especially when we played the US Military Academy.

On one occasion, one of our players, Julie Harwood, crashed into an opponent, and both fell to the ground in great pain with potentially serious leg injuries. A referee's time-out was called. Julie's father, Dr. David Harwood, was there. I knew him to be a top orthopedic surgeon in New Jersey and waved for him to come onto the field. He diagnosed both players and declared that while both were in considerable acute pain, and both had to leave the game, neither had a serious injury beyond needing a couple of days of general care.

My tour as a volunteer coach at the Academy phased out with the advent of lacrosse as a major sport there.

I don't recall how my next coaching position came about, but Scott Wagner, athletic director at the Williams School, a private college preparatory day school in New London, CT, hired me to be the head coach of the Williams School Girls' Varsity Lacrosse Team. Williams had an established program for both girls and boys. As coach of this team, I met many parents, mostly mothers. On occasion, I received an email message complaining about insufficient playing time. I would connect by phone or an in-person meeting and explain my reasoning and plans for the player, and that would generally be it. They were all quite reasonable.

We had two respectable seasons at Williams before Scott Wagner left Williams to become athletic director for a larger institution. Bern Macca, new to the school, replaced him at Williams. As the season got underway, it dawned on me that Bern wanted to replace me as she kept jotting down, for posterity, various crimes I was committing against humanity (alleged crimes). I wrote Bern and Mark Fader, head of the school, a letter saying that I would like to finish the season after which I would resign. I was replaced the next year by another white male, 50 years younger than me. I heard his name was Smoke…*That* I couldn't compete with.

I spent an abortive season as a certified referee (in Connecticut) of girls' lacrosse. It was physically too much for me. For the next three years, I was a volunteer coach in the youth program, the Lyme Ticks.

My son, Rich, and I ran a couple of summer lacrosse camps for girls during this period.

Then, in the spring of 2018, I wound up as head coach of the Old Saybrook Girls' Varsity Lacrosse team. That was the time I decided to send parents of the players a bulletin after each game via email. I wrote these bulletins the day after the game when I had a clearer perspective of what had transpired, and could almost replay the entire game in my head. Parents told me they appreciated receiving these bulletins, a practice which I continued until retirement.

John, the father of one of our players one season, felt a need to encourage and advise his daughter from the sidelines. While responsibility for fan behavior is only vaguely assigned to coaches, there are times, like away games, when there is no other person to deal with such matters. Such was the case in one game when John stationed himself in a particular place, not open to fans, in order to communicate better with his daughter on the field. I left my position in the coaching area and walked all the way around to where he was standing. I stood beside him for a minute or so without saying anything, and then muttered, "John, Julia doesn't need two coaches." John got the message, we subsequently became good friends, and his daughter did quite well that season and went on to play club lacrosse in college.

The sports culture at Old Saybrook was as good as it gets. Brendan Saunders became athletic director at Old Saybrook after the lost COVID season of 2020. He was a big supporter of the Girls' Varsity Lacrosse Program.

I decided to retire after the 2024 season. One more 40-minute bus ride to a game, then standing on my two feet for three hours (lacrosse coaches don't sit down), and then losing the game followed by a half-mile trek in a cold drizzle back to the bus, had become more of an ordeal than I wanted to contemplate.

Chapter 11
Technology Will Have a Positive Impact on the Game

Technology will make it practical for high school coaches to obtain much the same information that college coaches, with their larger budgets, can get. College coaches with a paid, trained staff can record important game stats that only the larger, better-staffed high schools can afford. The main difference will be statistics to measure defensive play and the performance of defense cohorts and individuals playing on defense. This same technology, as its use is expanded to include more and more schools and girls' lacrosse teams, will also have a positive impact on penalties, analysis of injuries, and potential rule changes, all for the better.

"Hudl" is that technology for schools today. Launched in 2007 in Indiana, Hudl claims to support 230,000 teams engaged in more than 40 different sports in 15 countries. Hudl's special cameras focus automatically on the action on the court or athletic field, recording every play for subsequent review and analysis. Each year, more and more of the action is recorded, analyzed, and shared automatically to provide coaches, athletes, and, to an extent, officials, with useful information.

In our 2024 season, Hudl was only available for one home game and one away game. The information was useful even in this truncated form. For the one home game, we used the service that included the automated analysis supplemented by experts behind the scenes.

Hudl has arrived on the scene at a time when lacrosse is expanding rapidly across the country (and much of the world), and therefore the demand for the information provided by Hudl is also increasing. I could see it would be helpful to plan practices and even to design specific drills. Perhaps its value for a specific coach will diminish over time, but ambitious student-athletes in high school should find it indispensable for self-improvement and showcases for college recruiters; that demand will grow with the sport.

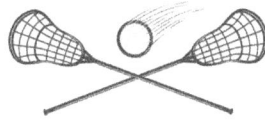

Chapter 12
Shooting

In the 2024 season, we had no trouble taking shots. Our scorekeeper, Hillary Sigersmith, kept good records of the shots taken by each individual player. We started the season with just 30% of our shots going in. We ended the season with just 30% of our shots going in. Throughout the season, we tried to improve that percentage. I think we got better, but so did our opponents, so we had to work hard just to stay even.

Whether it's boys' lacrosse or girls' lacrosse, I don't know of a really good practice drill to teach someone how to score a goal under intense defensive pressure. We can practice time and room shots, we can practice certain fakes, certain dodges that end with a shot, but when it comes to shooting in the heat of battle, nothing replaces a healthy scrimmage or an actual game against another team.

Shooting well in the midst of competitive pressure is largely self-taught. It is usually the result of years of play, not any single season. It's a rare athlete who can start playing lacrosse in high school and do well at scoring in her first season. A successful shot under duress may draw upon years of competitive play, muscle memory, split-second clear-headedness, and a predisposition to do whatever it takes to get off a good shot. Physical fitness, great agility, intense alertness, and a good sense of situational awareness are helpful and necessary, but not sufficient.

Players should learn to shoot hard and accurately.

Shooting is one area where a post-game analysis enabled by the likes of Hudl will have a significant impact. A coach could analyze every shot from which he or she can quantify generalizations such as:

"We shot when we were too far away from the goal."

"25% of our shots missed the goal entirely."

"When our attack faked high and shot low, the odds of a score improved."

"Their goalie was really good. She stopped our best shots…which were almost all high (or low)." Goalies tend to do better with one than the other.

"The last time we played against this team, their goalie had trouble with high shots. We should have remembered that."

"Half of our shots went right into the goalie's stick."

"We shot 34 times. Ten went in the goal, 8 of which were bounce shots; of the 24 shots that missed, only 3 were bounce shots…we should have bounced more of our shots."

Experienced players maintain a cool head when they are dodging toward the goal for a shot, and have the presence of mind to take careful aim at the largest patch of white net behind the goalie, or bounce it to one side of the goalie or the other.

We did what we could to help girls appreciate the magic of the bounce shot. We tried to persuade them that a bounce shot would get past the goalie twice as often as one thinks. Conversely, we declared that the goalie will stop twice as many shots that don't bounce as one thinks. We devoted plenty of time to practicing bounce shots. In scrimmages, we would handicap play by declaring, "The only way you can score from now on is with a bounce shot." No matter, it's just not the same as mortal combat against a worthy adversary. In the heat of a game, less-experienced players forget the probabilities and tend to shoot high at the goal instead of that imaginary spot on the ground just inside the crease. Players who learn to trust in the bounce shot and perfect it will have a powerful weapon in their arsenal.

We had 3 or 4 players who could score from the vicinity of the 8-meter arc. The rest had to get closer to the goal before shooting; we could accomplish this in one of two ways.

First, the attacker with the ball learns to run and dodge her way closer to the crease. Second, and most importantly from my perspective, the girl with the ball can make that short, crisp feed from behind, or from out in front, to a teammate nearer to the crease who has momentarily gotten herself open for a feed.

Getting open for a feed is a challenge in itself. Even when one player succeeds, does her teammate with the ball make the feed? We worked on this with modest success using predetermined pairs. E.g., "From now on, when Kendall has the ball out in front, her partner-attacker to get free for a feed on the crease is Lila." Kendall didn't have to feed Lila, but it helped that both girls knew what *might* happen.

Here are some other things we did to improve our shooting percentage.

1. Start at the sideline, facing across the field, with two lines in a competitive ground ball drill on about the 20-yard line. The girl who gets the ball runs to the goal, fakes high, and shoots low (or some facsimile thereof). As there is no defender against the shooter, it was optional for one of our goalies to be in the goal for this drill.

2. Time and room shots from the 8-meter arc (See the photos that demonstrate this shot in Chapter 2). Alternate between shooting high and bouncing.

3. Free position penalty shots in which the player face-dodges toward the goal, jigs left, and shoots off to the right (the strong side for right-handers) for a shot. Players should reach the center line of the field a few feet in front of the crease with enough time to fake a shot to the upper left, and then shoot to the upper right, just over the goalie's left shoulder (or, better yet, bounce the shot to the lower right for a changeup…goalies have good memories of where specific players have been shooting). Goalie in the goal for these (See the photos that demonstrate this maneuver in Chapter 2).

4. Same as above, but with, say, a red kerchief tied through the net in the upper right-hand corner (over the goalie's left shoulder) of the goal as a target; extra credit if the shooter hits the kerchief.
5. Running the gauntlet: A string of 5 "defenders" place themselves along any yard line across the field, spaced about ten yards apart. The girl with the ball must run past these defenders but cannot go outside the two adjacent five-yard lines running parallel across the field. When this drill is first introduced, the defenders stay in one place, using their sticks to poke the stick of the ball carrier only if she leaves it unprotected. Once everyone gets the hang of it, the defenders can be more aggressive, going to their left or right to stop the ball carrier, letting her go once she's passed them. The five defenders index their way along, then get in line to run the gauntlet themselves.

To improve shooting accuracy and results in general, there is nothing like a good wall or bounce-back at home.

Note: In a settled offense, we lined up with two players behind the goal, one on either side. Whenever a scoring play started, it was the responsibility of any member of the attack not engaged in the scoring play to take up a strategic position behind the goal in case the shot missed the goal, and run it out (be the player closest to the ball as it goes out of bounds) to retain possession. If we had a player in the game on offense who knew she was unlikely to score, she would remain behind the goal, ready to run out any shots that missed the goal.

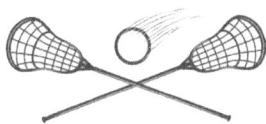

Chapter 13
Penalties

The girls' lacrosse rulebook is published by the National Federation of State High School Associations. The Rules Committee for Girls' Lacrosse in 2024 was comprised of a publisher and editor from NFHS plus 11 volunteers from around the country representing coaches, officials, administrators, and USA Lacrosse. A fresh copy of the rules book is issued each year. It is complete and highlights changes from the previous year. Coaches and officials in CT are required to attend a session before each season in which changes to the rule are discussed.

Patti Klecha-Porter, a veteran lacrosse umpire and head coach of the Wesleyan field hockey team since 1985 has chaired this discussion in all six of the seasons I coached at Old Saybrook. Patti has been inducted into the Hall of Fame of both field hockey and lacrosse. She officiated at one or two of our games each year. We were fortunate to have competent, impartial referees in our league. Even though Patti could make the occasional mistake, she was indisputably the best.

It's unfortunate when a referee and a player get into some kind of a tangle. A player may feel that a referee is out to get her. She may be right. The player may have earned special treatment in a prior game by being disrespectful to the referee in some way. In the heat of battle, a player may utter a curse word impulsively; referees hear things inaudible from the sidelines. In a tough game, the players might come off the field during a time-out and complain about the referees. In such cases, we listened sincerely to the players…and then we told them, "Deal with it."

One thing we learned the hard way: If a referee does something egregiously wrong like pulling out a red card when he or she meant a yellow card, the time to deal with it is right then and there. A yellow card means the player goes into the penalty box for two minutes; a red card means the player is expelled from the current game *and the next game, without a substitution*, a huge difference.

We spent much time helping our players understand the difference between a proper and an improper check on an opponent's stick to dislodge the ball. If the opponent is cradling the stick vertically and the only way to hit her stick is by checking close to her head, we instructed our team to forget the check. Don't do it. It's not worth the penalty or, more importantly, the chances of inflicting injury. Proper checks, on the other hand, at roughly waist level, swift snappy checks, in and out quickly, down and away from the opponent, could result in a clean turnover, safely and without penalty.

There are only a few rules that were troublesome for me as a coach, those that protect too much, and those that don't protect enough. Here is an example of each.

When a goalie (or her parents) must pay $200–$400 for a helmet, a helmet that protects the head and throat of the player, why penalize a shooter for hitting the goalie in the helmet? It's called "dangerous propelling." The calls can be, and are, highly subjective and inconsistent between referees. There is no such penalty in boy's lacrosse. Aren't their heads just as valuable and just as vulnerable as girls? And don't boys have a harder shot than girls? Some referees overuse this penalty in the name of safety and deny shooters goals that they legitimately earned.

On the other hand, when a defending player other than the goalie gets hit on the head with a hard shot, the shooter gets a yellow card ("dangerous propelling") and is in the penalty box for two minutes. *Two minutes* out of the game in exchange for a blow to the head that could possibly affect the girl who has been hit for a long time.

If a member of the offensive team hits a defender in the head with a shot, that shooter should receive a red card, be expelled from the game, and be disallowed from playing in the next game. Only in that way will the girl taking the shot think twice before shooting, and instead, possibly get a free shot for "shooting space" called on the defender ["shooting space" is called when a defender is in the way of the shooter between her and the goal, and is more than a stick's length away from the shooter, thus denying the shooter a clear shot at the goal; the better referees are adept at recognizing shooting space instantly and blowing the whistle in time for the shooter to abort her shot].

We experienced such a shot to the head of our top defensive player, Grace Desmond, during our 2024 season. The incident was captured on the Hudl video which we obtained some days after the game. A player on the North Branford team took a shot at the goal and hit Grace square on her forehead. I didn't see it until we were able to watch it on Hudl. The ball is shown heading for Grace, hitting her squarely, and bouncing off at high speed. Mercifully, Grace was unhurt; at least, that's what she told me later.

Did Grace inadvertently step in the way of the shot, which should therefore have been stopped by the referee's whistle, and a shooting space penalty called on her? This is certainly possible, but Grace was highly accomplished when it came to avoiding the shooting space penalty.

The shooter from North Branford got a yellow card and was out of the game for two minutes.

With Hudl-like information, analysts will be better equipped to perform post-mortems, and thereby improve coach, player, injury analysis, and referee training.

Chapter 14
Confidence, Poise, and Mental Toughness

To me, a player has reached her stride when she can enter the toughest games, confident of playing her best, poised in combat, and mentally tough enough to deal with any other problems in her life. She should be so in touch with the moment that she is clear-headed and alert to split-second opportunities and is an inspiration to her teammates at all times.

Some players can do well mainly at defense; keeping opponents away from the goal; deflecting shots that otherwise might have gone in; making good, safe, and effective checks on opponents' sticks; sliding or switching seamlessly and effortlessly with teammates. They are tough on ground balls and can run and dodge and pass on clearing plays. They are good at blocking passes. They can run and dodge their way downfield into their attacking zone.

They make great defenders, but they may lose their cool on offense. The prospect of scoring a goal may overwhelm them for an instant. They can be momentarily disoriented when confronted by an able defender on the other team. They know exactly where to be when playing defense, but they're not as comfortable, or poised, when on offense.

Other players may do well mainly on offense. They thrive on the unknowns of offense. The tougher the defender, the harder they drive and shoot or assist. They like to score, and they like to assist. They like to control the ball. They are good at short bursts of speed, and they see, sense, and seize opportunities to pass and score instantaneously in otherwise impossible situations. They can spin, dodge, lose their balance, bounce off opponents, and leap and shoot, or assist, while in mid-air.

When the other team gets the ball, though, their shoulders may droop, disappointed that the momentum to score has just shifted to the other team. They react more slowly, become disoriented, and lose their poise.

Then there are the players who will do well in just about all of the above situations including the draw. These are mainly midfielders. They can run fast…all day long. They know where to be and how to react at all times in any situation. When appropriate, they get low, in an athletic stance, ready to dart in any direction. They know a ground ball can still be recovered even after an opponent gets the ball in her stick, momentarily leaving it open for a safe, snappy check. When a veteran midfielder gets the ball in her stick, teammates and coaches relax, knowing that this ball, one way or another, will now be safely transported down-field into their attacking zone.

Goalies are in a world of their own. They have to be uniquely intent on stopping hard, deceptive shots. They should be alert to interceptions around the goal and crease. They should be great stick handlers capable of cradling, running, dodging, and passing down-field.

Players can learn and develop in any one of these positions over their four years in high school. If they don't make it their freshman or sophomore year, they can still achieve poise and confidence by their junior or senior year. They may or may not play in college, but as the sport has grown, so have opportunities to continue lacrosse on college club teams, if not varsity or junior varsity. Club teams at some colleges have serious schedules and travel far and wide for games, much the same as the varsity team, but without the same level of stress and commitment of time and effort. Such opportunities present themselves to players who reach a level of poise and self-confidence in whatever position they play in high school.

Mental toughness should not be confused with mental health. When it comes to mental health, I defer to Ann and Paul Dagle, founders of the Brian Dagle Foundation in honor of their son, Brian.

Each of the past few years, we have participated in the Dagle Foundations' "Lax2Live" program after a selected home game. Brian was an avid lacrosse player at Castleton College, VT, when he took his life at age 19. Brian's father, Paul Dagle, presides at a brief presentation at half-time in memory of Brian, in support of those who may need help, and encouragement to student-athletes to seek help should they find themselves in a depressed state. It is a sensitive well-designed program that our team always supported.

Brian's mother, Ann, a self-taught, nationally recognized expert in grief counseling, runs the foundation which expresses the following on its website:

"This Foundation was created as a way to share and continue Brian's immense love—his love for life, for family and for friends. Brian died by suicide in November of 2011.

"On that devastating day, our family, Brian's friends and the community in which we live felt as though we were hit by a tsunami, and in many ways, we were. We were plagued by the question of how this seemingly happy, friendly, smiling young man could take his own life. But we now know that behind his warm, infectious, beautiful smile was a young man suffering in silence from depression and anxiety; a young man who didn't realize that it was okay to ask for help."

As coaches, we must be on the lookout for troubling behavior. If we sense something that bothers us, our job is to report the matter to the school's athletic director who, as a senior member of the school administration, is able to raise awareness of such with trained counselors.

When it comes to mental toughness, I liked what Dr. Colleen Hacker, professor of kinesiology at Pacific Lutheran University, had to say:

"Mental toughness is a skill. Mental toughness has gotten a bad rap. That doesn't mean playing injured. Or denying your feelings, or not engaging in mental health…Mental toughness is just about how you respond to adversity, difficulties, setbacks, and failure. And it is a skill you can develop, but you cannot develop it when things are going well."

I witnessed a lot of what I would call mental toughness in the Women's Lacrosse Team at the Coast Guard Academy. The admissions departments at our military academies must look for mental toughness in their applicants. If the applicants don't have (enough of) it when they enter, they soon will after they have survived the stress and indignities of plebe life.

Two of our best players tore their ACLs as sophomores in off-season lacrosse and missed playing regular-season lacrosse in their junior years. Both recovered physically, emotionally, and mentally and enjoyed highly successful senior years. One, Carrington (Gillie) Hartt, was co-captain of a team that went undefeated in the regular season. The other was Laura Day, co-captain of a team that won the Shoreline League championship. Both young women went on to play lacrosse in college, one on the college varsity team, and the other on the college club team. Both developed a mental toughness that will serve them well throughout life.

Coach Wooden placed "confidence" and "poise" next to the top of his pyramid; I would add "mental toughness."

At the very top, Wooden listed "Competitive Excellence."

Chapter 15
The 2024 Season

Old Saybrook 22 - Montville 14 (unofficial scrimmage score)

When the season finally got underway with a scrimmage against Montville, on March 27, we still had 15 players, with 6 from the previous season; for the other 9 players, Monville was their introduction to high school lacrosse. The roster on March 27 was the only official thing (see Figure 1).

Both coaches used this scrimmage as a serious practice, with spontaneous time-outs by the coaches to make coaching points. The final score was an unofficial 22–14, in our favor. Some post-game stats that jumped out at me:

1. All by herself, and even though she did not do the draw herself but was one of the "demons" at the circle, Amelia retrieved 11 of the draws while Kendall got 7 and Ayla 3. The draw demons got 21 of the 26 draws for a remarkable 81%. This was absolutely a harbinger of things to come.

2. Ayla fired 33 shots at the goal, netting 10 of them. It was clear that Ayla was also fired up for this season of her junior year. The thought crossed my mind that Ayla might become overly anxious to score goals at the possible expense of good team play; I need not have worried as Ayla, on her own, developed a good balance during the remainder of the season between her personal ambitions (she scored her 200th goal as a junior before

the regular season ended) and her ambition for her team (she was co-captain). All told, Old Saybrook threw the ball at the goal 63 times, scoring on 22 of them, or 35%. It was good that we took a lot of shots, but we should have scored on more of them. We had much work to do on shooting accuracy.

3. The team got better relative to the opposition as the game progressed, scoring 5 goals in the first half and 17 in the second.

4. Of Old Saybrook's 22 goals, 12 were assisted by 6 of the 7 members of our offensive cohort; Lila Cadley, the 7th member, did not assist but scored 3 times. This argued well for a balanced offensive cohort.

5. Our defense appeared weak in this contest; predictably, we had lots of work to do on defense. While we didn't record "successful clears" in this game, this was another discernible vulnerability at this early stage.

Because we had so many players out for spring vacation (only 4 players turned out for one practice), our next two scheduled games against Waterford and North Branford were postponed until later in the season.

Old Saybrook 12 – Morgan 9 (Shoreline League, both teams are Class S, for Small)

Our first official game of the season was also our first Shoreline Conference game, against Morgan (the town of Clinton's high school). We could always expect a good, hard-fought, close game against the well-coached Morgan team. In the event, however, Old Saybrook won handily, 12–9

The draw demons came up with 16 out of 25 draws (64%), 5 of our offensive cohort scored while 6 assisted. Out of a total of 36 shots fired at the goal, 12 went in for 36%. We could see modest progress on offense; our defense did well against a worthy opponent.

I felt we played well and that our season was off to a pretty good start.

Old Saybrook 2 - Fitch 12 (Non-league, Class L for Large)

Lest we harbor any illusions of grandeur, however, our game against the out-of-league Fitch team (Groton), was a reminder that we had a long way to go. While we did not expect to win or even have a close game (Fitch trotted out 22 players, each one, it seemed, capable of passing and catching under pressure), to lose 12–2 showed that we could be intimidated by a marginally superior team; in other words, when we went up against a better team, in this instance, we played badly. We took 22 shots at the goal, scoring only twice (10%). Only the draw demons did well, snagging 8 out of 16.

In the Shoreline League, the athletic directors determined the schedule (or at least in our case). I always liked to see non-league teams that were better than our team, not worse; we would learn more by playing against better teams. Against Fitch, we learned what humble pie tastes like.

Old Saybrook 5 - New Fairfield 16 (Non-league, class M, for Medium)

Our team has traditionally been energized by cold rain and wind. This game, another non-league game, was no exception. Trouble is, the New Fairfield girls were equally fired up. In a game that was almost all defense for Old Saybrook, Cali did her best in the goal with 16 saves. With four players missing, we were one player short for this game, so we put our best foot forward with a four-person midfield comprised of the three draw demons (Amelia, Kendall, and Ayla) plus Claire.

Our attack included Sylvie (an experienced freshman), Julia (a relatively inexperienced freshman), and our second-string goalie, Erin. Unbeknownst to me, our captains, knowing we were at a serious disadvantage in this game, had set a target of scoring at least five goals, no matter what New Fairfield did. Though we lost 16–5, when the fifth goal was scored, no one was more surprised than the other team when our gang let out a hearty cheer. Only our "midfielders" scored: Kendall scored twice; Ayla, Amelia, and Claire had one apiece.

Old Saybrook 20 – Valley 6 (League)

In this game, the Old Saybrook Rams played their best game so far, both on defense and offense. By this time, Grace had developed the defensive cohort to the point where they represented, as a group, an "impenetrable" wall in front of the goal, a scene we would recognize often during the season.

Ayla clearly established herself as a target for our opponents to "face-guard" the rest of the season as she scored 8 times, a career-high.

Valley has always had a competitive team, so to have such a one-sided encounter was both surprising and a bit disappointing. I was pleased that we had played up, though, and not down.

Old Saybrook 11 – Haddam-Killingworth (HK) 7 (League)

With Cali, our first-string goalie, away, this was Erin's first opportunity in the goal for an entire game. My earlier fears were erased as Erin had 5 good saves and made several key clearing passes. Our defense was solid against an otherwise tough team, and cleared the ball successfully 12 out of 13 times; on the other side, Old Saybrook stopped 30% of HK's clears. The draw demons retrieved the ball on 15 out of 22 attempts. HK scored on 47% of their tries versus our relatively poor success rate of 29%. We still had a long way to go with scoring accuracy.

Old Saybrook 17 – Cromwell 4 (League)

The Old Saybrook Rams dominated against the less-experienced, relatively new, Cromwell Panthers and their new coach. Not sure we learned much, but one good thing: despite the lopsided score, we did not play badly.

Old Saybrook 6 – Old Lyme 8 (League)

This was a crunch game for us. I thought Old Lyme was destined to win the league championship this year with many experienced and very competitive seniors. Both teams played well on defense throughout, keeping the score low on both sides. Cali was outstanding in the goal with 18 saves and two interceptions. On offense, freshman Ainsley scored once with two assists. No one felt badly about their performance in this game. I thought we were pretty psyched for the next game.

Old Saybrook 3 – Waterford 17 (Non-league, class M)

Less than 18 hours after losing to Old Lyme, the next morning the Rams faced off against Waterford. Wham! Waterford outdid us in every category of play…the draw, scoring, defending, clearing, and riding clears. I had done no scouting of this team, or I might have seen that our varsity could have had a decent game against their junior varsity.

Old Saybrook 10 – North Branford 11 (League)

As North Branford subsequently won our league championship against Old Lyme, we lost this game to the best team in our league by one goal. Old Saybrook trailed the entire game, tying it up at 10–10 with just minutes to go. It was a brutal game in which Grace, our lead defender, was hit in the head more than once by over-zealous opponents. Toward the end, a North Branford attacker hit the pipe of the goal and it bounced almost straight down, just outside of the imaginary goal face; it was therefore a geometric impossibility that the ball had entered the goal…but the referee called it a score. Our gang was ready for a re-match…which, because of our player shortage during spring break and the resulting postponements, was now our very next game.

Old Saybrook 13 – North Branford 9 (League)

The date was **May 2**. Since it was the high watermark of our season, we'll revert to this game in the next chapter.

Old Saybrook 6 – Old Lyme 14 (League)

Old Lyme ran over us in this game. To me, it was inexplicable; I had no explanation, let alone excuse, for our poor performance in this game. The draw demons netted 50%, but our defense was suddenly tentative for the entire game. Cali Morelli missed this game as she had other priorities, but that was no excuse as Erin did well in the goal with 9 impressive saves. Two other players, Ainsley and Julia, also missed this game, so we had no substitute; luckily, none was needed. I felt demoralized and feared the team might be, as well.

Old Saybrook 14 – Haddam-Killingworth 13 (League)

The Old Saybrook Rams narrowly led the entire game. The draw demons were back in stride with 17 of 31 draws or 55%. Kendall had her best game of the season so far with 6 goals and one assist. Claire, Amelia, and Lila also scored. It was a hard-fought, exciting game with the Rams displaying considerable poise as they held on to their slim margin for the requisite 48 minutes. Against this much-improved team from HK, it felt good to be back in a groove with just three games left to the season, all in our league. By this time, we needed just one more win to lock up a berth in the league playoffs.

Figure 6

Here is the score card for the team at the end of the regular season:

Player Offense	Goals	Assists	Points	Saves
Ayla D'Anna	61	28	89	
Kendall Dobratz	44	6	50	
Claire Cassella	24	14	38	
Lila Cadley	29	8	37	
Amelia Sigersmith	10	23	33	
Ainsley Sigersmith	6	14	20	
Sylvie Webber	8	4	12	
Grace Desmond		1	1	
Goalies				
Cali Morelli				116
Erin Fiorelli				18
Totals: Rams (opponents)	192 (vs 156)	98	280	

Looking back at the regular season, we took a lot of shots but failed to score on too many of them. We knew our shooting accuracy was poor. We worked hard to remedy the problem but never did.

Old Saybrook 12 – Morgan 8 (League)

There was no such thing as an easy win over Morgan. To add to the drama, the game was played at night under the lights of the town of Clinton's Indian River Athletic Complex. Every player on the Old Saybrook team did her job as the team dominated on draws, ripped into the Morgan offense causing broken plays, and scored on 12 out of 35 shots fired. The score at halftime was 10–2. The Rams might be excused if they let up in the second half. There were too many penalties on both sides. It was our toughest game of the season to win, and even tougher on Morgan to lose; Morgan's star player, Maeve Madura, scored 4 times, and wanted more, but was turned away by Grace and her teammates. Except for the penalties, which may have been in part a function of the referee's concerns for safety in such a heated contest, it was a game for Old Saybrook's team to savor on the late bus home.

Old Saybrook 16 – Cromwell 4 (League)

With the draw demons spearing 17 out of 24 draws (71%), this game was never in doubt against an improved team from Cromwell. Old Saybrook scored on 16 out of 56 total shots on goal (29%), however, a lousy (and troubling) percentage at this stage in the season.

Old Saybrook 16 – Valley Regional 7 (League)

This was Senior Day for Old Saybrook's lone senior, Amelia. Before the game, we recognized Amelia and also Valley's lone senior, Rowan Pilon. Both girls had played together with the Lyme Ticks (as it happened, I had coached both of them in that capacity). Both represented their teams and the sport of lacrosse superbly over the years. If we had kept better records over the years, we could show how much Amelia and Rowan had each contributed to their team during their time as high school players; as one of the best crease rollers ever, Rowan would have been one of the league's highest scorers, and I'm almost certain Amelia would have scored a record of assists, ground balls, and center draws. It was a day of ceremonials as Ayla scored her 200th career goal as a junior.

Old Saybrook finished the regular season in third place behind Old Lyme and North Branford with 9 wins and 3 losses, 2 of those losses against Old Lyme, 1 loss, and 1 win against the eventual league champion, North Branford.

The post-season games

The post-season requires its own kind of mental preparedness. A team and its coaches eager to do well in the regular season have to prepare mentally as well as physically for the long road to a good season; in our case, the season involved 16 games in 9 weeks. By the end, a team will have expended much physical and emotional energy. Then it has to immediately pick itself up for the post-season games. I think it takes a conscious effort on the part of coaches, captains, and players to pace themselves during the regular season and then muster the confidence, enthusiasm, and energy to do well in the post-season games. I'm not sure that the Old Saybrook team was capable of regrouping and firing itself up for this particular post-season. I wasn't as prepared as I would have liked, and I also knew that my attitude, especially if it was ever-so-slightly negative, or just not as positive as I could be, could have a corresponding negative effect on the team.

The Shoreline League Championship tournament began with four (out of our seven) teams in the semifinals. Old Lyme was pitted against Morgan and Old Saybrook faced North Branford…both pairings for the third time. Old Lyme beat Morgan, and North Branford beat Old Saybrook. In an upset in the finals, North Branford beat Old Lyme.

Old Saybrook 8 – North Branford 10 (League semi-final)

On paper, this was not a bad game for the Rams. We were leading by two goals as the end of the first half approached. North Branford scored twice, however, before the half-time whistle blew to even the score at 5–5, thus stealing the momentum away from Old Saybrook. North Branford's player of the year, Keana Criscuolo, scored 6 times with 3 assists as if to underscore that she truly deserved this honor.

Old Saybrook 13 – Wheeler 15 (State championship, round of sixteen)

For the State championship, Old Saybrook drew Wheeler in the first round of sixteen. Our scouting turned up the information that we would face another star player, Sophia Gouveia (Wouldn't you know it? I had coached Sophia in the Ticks when she was ten or so). Surely, we would be able to contain such a star. While we didn't play great, we didn't do badly, but Sophia managed to snag 11 out of 32 draws all by herself and went on to score 8 times with two assists; this was the second time, two games in a row, when an opponent had possibly her best game ever against us.

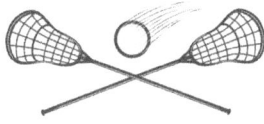

Chapter 16
May 2

By the second of May, seven weeks into our season, our team was performing well on the five basic functions. At the top of our list were our "draw demons," Amelia, Kendall, and Ayla. They excelled consistently, always getting more than their share of the draws against the teams in our league. Our ability to control the ball on offense had improved greatly; we were no longer in a hurry to shoot every time we had the ball, and the percentage of the time we scored when we had possession was also improving. If we still had weak spots, it was riding the clears and shooting accuracy. On the other hand, we got better and better with our own clears. Finally, increasingly during the season, our defense led by Grace Desmond had done much to deprive our opponents of goals they would have otherwise made. We were in a good place for this game, and all fifteen players showed up.

Kendall started the ball rolling with the first goal of the game 1 minute and 47 seconds into the first quarter. Amelia scored two minutes later, then Kendall for two more and Lila for one, making it 5–0 before North Branford had scored a goal. Keana Criscuolo scored for North Branford to end the quarter. In the second quarter, Lila and Amelia scored once each while North Branford scored three more times making it 7–4 as the end of the half neared.

Up to that point, the Old Saybrook Rams had not made a single mistake on offense. Out of 12 draws so far in the first half, the Rams' draw demons had succeeded with 11 of them. As the half-time horn neared, I was holding my breath, waiting to see if either team might score before the half ended. If North Branford could score again, and not Old Saybrook, the half would end at 7–5, with the momentum shifting in North Branford's favor. If Old Saybrook could score again, but not North Branford, the half would end at 8–4, with Old Saybrook holding on to the momentum. With 52 seconds remaining in the first half, freshman Sylvie Webber, who had not scored in the previous two games, came at the goal from the left side, face-dodged once, maybe twice, and scored. The best half of any game I had ever coached or played in came to an end with the score 8–4.

The two teams traded 5 goals each in the second half to end the game 13–9 for Old Saybrook.

Not without significance, our opponents incurred 28 penalties versus 11 for Old Saybrook.

From the stat sheet (Figure 7), note that the scoring by Old Saybrook was evenly distributed across the offensive seven; six of the seven had scored. Kendall scored four times, Ayla, Lila, Claire, and Amelia all scored twice, and Sylvie scored once. It is hard to defend against an offensive cohort on a day when any one of them can score.

The North Branford coach, players, and even some of their fans went berserk…unable to accept the fact that on this day, **May 2**, 2024, fifteen girls from Old Saybrook…nine of them new to the high school level of play just a few weeks earlier… a team I was privileged to coach… were simply the better team.

Figure 7
Thursday, May 2, 2024
Old Saybrook 13 — North Branford 9

Results as entered in the Official Score Book (Players in *italics* were new to the team this year)

NR	Starting Team	Shots on Goal	Goals	Assists	Goals in First Half
16	Kendall Dobratz	6	4		3
2	*Claire Cassella*	5	2	3	
1	Lila Cadley	5	2	2	2
18	Amelia Sigersmith, capt	3	2		2
8	Ayla D'Anna, capt	7	2		
12	*Sylvie Webber*	1	1		1
16	*Ainsley Sigersmith*	1			
7	Grace Desmond, capt				
19	*Zoe Parakilas*				
10	*Emma Courtright*				
3	*Caroline Adams*				
4	Cali Morelli Saves = 5 + 2 = 7				
	TOTALS	28	13	5	8
	Substitutes				
	Erin Fiorelli				
	Julia Maselli				
	Felicia Lombard				
	North Branford (a measure of how well Old Saybrook's defense played)		9		4

DRAW DEMONS

Amelia	9
Kendall	6
Ayla	3
Total	**18 out of 26**

SCOREKEEPERS

Hillary Sigersmith

Denise Dobratz

COACHES

Dick Shriver

Rich Shriver

Emily Haviland

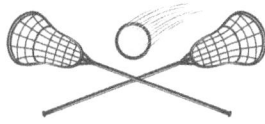

Epilogue

Co-captains and juniors Grace and Ayla made first-team All-State; sophomore Kendall made second-team.

Coaching became a calling for me when I began to feel that we were adding real, lasting value to the lives of the amazing young people on our teams.

What I like about the Girls' Game (without helmets): There is a place for finesse in the sport much like what used to characterize Boys' Lacrosse before the mass production of sticks comprised of exotic composites, and the resultant emphasis on power.

Congratulations to the new Head Coach of Girls' Varsity Lacrosse at Old Saybrook High School starting in 2025: Coach Rich Shriver.

Appendix A
Weekly Bulletins for the 2024 Season

Note: The bulletins that follow are reproduced here exactly as they were sent to parents, with misspellings among other errors.

Girls' Varsity Lacrosse...Bulletin # 1...Week ending April 6, 2024

League record	W - 1	L-0
Overall	W-1	L-1

With 6 returning players and 9 players (8 freshmen and 1 sophomore) new to the team this season, things are bound to be challenging. In our first league game, against Morgan (Clinton), the Rams won, 12–5. In our first non-league game, against Fitch (Groton), the Rams lost 2–14. It was quite a change-up.

The Morgan Game (12-5): Morgan scored the first two goals while Old Saybrook got its bearings. With mostly veteran players on attack and midfield, and mostly new players on defense, Saybrook dominated the center draws, coming up with 16 out of 24 tries, or 64%. On offense, Saybrook scored 12 times with 36 shots on goal for a success rate of 33%; 6 of Saybrook's 12 goals were assisted for a very respectable success rate of 50%.

Junior Kendall Dobratz led in scoring with 4 goals and an assist. Co-captain Ayla D'Anna was second high scorer with 3 goals and an assist. Freshman Claire Courtright had 2 goals and an assist as did junior Lila Cadley. Ainsley Sigersmith, freshman, tallied once with an assist while co-captain and the team's lone senior, Amelia Sigersmith, had 3 assists. Freshman Sylvie Webber played well on offense behind the goal. On defense, freshmen Julia Maselli, Zoe Parakilas, and Caroline Adams...along with sophomore Emma Courtright...all had the thrill of winning their first high school game. In the goal, Cali Morelli had 6 saves.

The Fitch Game (2–14): A very disciplined and experienced Fitch team overwhelmed Old Saybrook with its steady defense, effective clearing and penetrating shots. Saybrook took 20 shots on goal, scoring only twice. Kendall and Ayla both scored once each, with an assist by Claire. Co-captain Grace Desmond and freshman Zoe Parakilas were standouts on defense. Goalie Cali Morelli had 8 saves.

For your coaches:

Dick Shriver
860 671 1634
rhsusa@gmail.com

Girls' Varsity Lacrosse...Bulletin # 2...Week ending April 13, 2024

League record	W - 1	L–0
Overall	W–1	L–2

As they have demonstrated in the past, it seems the Old Saybrook Girls' Varsity Lacrosse Team thrives on cold...rain...and wind; trouble is, the out-of-our-league New Fairfield Girls' Varsity Lacrosse Team was equally energized by foul weather. These two teams met yesterday in a spirited contest that ended 16–5 for New Fairfield; as NF is a larger opponent with more experienced players, the Rams had set realistic expectations for this game, which they may have exceeded.

It was a game of defense for the Rams. Cali Morelli outdid herself with 16 saves. Protecting the goal were the Rams' usual defenders led by Grace Desmond and supported by Emma Courtright and Zoe Parakilas; the remaining defenders included Amelia Sigersmith, Ayla D'Anna, Kendall Dobratz and Claire Casella. This able foursome moved up and down the field as a four-person midfield as the team was one player short for this game, or eleven players total.

The Rams attack was made up of just three players, Sylvie Webber (normal), Julia Maselli (new to the position) and Erin Fiorello (not only new to the position, but normally a goalie for the Rams; it was Erin's first appearance [but not her last] on the field with a conventional stick).

The first half ended with New Fairfield leading 10-2. The game ended with an improved and psyched Old Saybrook team and a respectable 6-3 second half, for a final score of 16-5. Kendall was high scorer with 2 goals; Amelia and Ayla had a goal and an assist apiece, and Claire had one goal.

With this non-league game as good preparation for upcoming games, the Rams now face Valley in an away game at 3:45 Tuesday, and a night game at home with Haddam-Killingworth at 7:00 Thursday. Hope to see everyone there!

For the coaches:

Dick Shriver
860 671 1634
rhsusa@gmail.com

Girls' Varsity Lacrosse...Bulletin # 3...Week ending April 20, 2024

League record	W - 3	L-0
Overall	W-3	L-2

With Spring break finally in the rear-view mirror, the Rams had their first real week of lacrosse for the 2024 season. It turned out well with two more league wins, 20–6 over Valley, and 11–7 over Haddam-Killingworth. As we play both of these teams again, both will have improved, so the past can be a misleading indication of the future. Nonetheless, the Rams played well in both games, and they, too, can improve.

Valley: 20–6: The Valley game was significant in that the Rams played a balanced game, good defense and good offense. Grace Desmond sparked the defense, limiting valley's formidable player, Rowen Pilon, to three goals. Grace was backed up time and again by upcoming defenders Zoe Parakilass, Julia Maselli, and Emma Courtright. In the goal, Cali Morelli had 5 saves. This defensive unit has come a long way in a short time.

On offense, Ayla D'Anna had a career record with 8 goals and an assist...also establishing her as a target for possible face-guarding in future games. Lila Cadley and Claire Casella turned in best-ever results with 5 goals/2 assists and 3 goals/5 assists respectively. Amelia Sigersmith accounted for 3 assists. Sylvie Webber scored twice with one assist. Kendall Dobratz had 1 goal and 1 assist, and Ainsley Sigersmith scored once.

Haddam-Killingworth: 11–7:
With the Rams' first string goalie away on official duties, Erin Fiorelli had her first opportunity to defend the Old Saybrook goal for an entire game...and defend it she did, with five important saves and several equally important clearing passes. A tight game throughout, the Rams' defense never let up.

The school's "Hudl" video system enables us to obtain stats for home games that we do not gather ordinarily. Here are some interesting stats from this game.

On clears, the Rams succeeded 93% of the time. When it was time for H-K to clear the ball, the Rams' attack stopped H-K's clear 30% of the time, leaving H-K with a 70% clear rate.

At the center draw, Old Saybrook's crack draw team of Amelia, Ayla and Kendall, came up with an overwhelming 68%. Old Saybrook out-possessed H-K 64% to 36% of the time. On shots at goal, however, the Rams scored a modest 29% of the time versus H-K's 47%.

Ayla was high scorer with 4 goals. Kendall, Lila Cadley and Sylvie Webber all tallied twice each. Amelia and Ainsley Sigersmith assisted 3 times each, for a total of 6, or more than half of the Rams' 11 goals.

Next Week: The Rams face Cromwell in an away game on Tuesday, April 23, at 3:00. On Friday the 26th, Old Saybrook faces off against undefeated Old Lyme at 4:00, also away. On Saturday April 27, the Rams play a non-league game at home against Waterford at 10:00.

For the coaches: Dick Shriver

Girls' Varsity Lacrosse...Week # 4 ending April 27, 2024

League record	W - 4	L–1
Overall	W–4	L–4

Cromwell 17–4

The Rams dominated the larger but less-experienced Cromwell team. Ayla D'Anna scored 6 goals, Lila Cadley had 4 goals and an assist, and Claire Cassella scored 4 times. Amelia Sigersmith had one goal and an assist, and Sylvie Webber scored twice with an assist. In the goal, Cali Morelli had 4 saves.

Old Lyme 6 - 8

Old Saybrook played its best game this year against Old Lyme, currently number 1 in the Shoreline League. It was a game in which the defensive teams on both sides kept the scores in check. Under the leadership of Co-captain Grace Desmond, her cadre of defensive players, all new to the Rams this year...

Zoe Parakilass, Emma Courtright, Caroline Adams, Felicia Lombard and Julia Maselli...slowed Old Lyme's scoring machine while the Rams' goalie, Cali Morelli, topped off two interceptions with a stunning 18 saves. Old Saybrook's top scorer, also new to the team this year, was freshman Ainsley Sigersmith with 1 goal and 2 assists. Claire Cassella and Kendall Dobratz scored twice each, while co-captains Ayla D'Anna and Amelia Sigersmith had 3 assists and 1 goal, respectively.

Waterford 3-17
It was not so much a difference in individual abilities as it was a difference in team play and deep experience in scoring, riding, clearing and defending. Eighteen hours after their game against Old Lyme, the Rams were on the field the next morning against a much superior Waterford team. Goals were hard to come by as Amelia, Lila and Claire each scored once and Ayla assisted once. Cali had 8 saves while Erin Fiorelli turned away another 4 shots.

This coming week, the Rams have two days to re-set and prepare themselves for another challenging week. The team faces North Branford twice, Monday evening at 6:00 away, and Thursday at 4:00 at home, followed by their second game against Old Lyme, also at home, on Saturday morning, May 4, at 11:00.

For the coaches

Coach Dick Shriver

Girls' Varsity Lacrosse...Week # 5 ending May 5, 2024

League record	W - 5	L–3
Overall	W–5	L–6

Lost to North Branford 10-11, Monday, April 29

North Branford took an early lead as Old Saybrook struggled to get its footing. But get it, it did, as the Rams evened the score at 10 all with just minutes to go. North Branford kept an edge on center draws and clearing percentage, however. Grace Desmond led a strong defensive effort throughout despite being pummeled by desperate Thunderbirds from North Branford. Cali Morelli's 16 saves also contributed to a game that nearly ended in a tie. On offense, Ayla D'Anna was high scorer with 3 goals, and 4 assists. Kendall Dobratz and Claire Cassella had two goals each, Lila Cadley scored once and assisted once, while Amelia and Ainsley Sigersmith each had one goal apiece. It was a close one... maybe next time?

Beat North Branford 13-9, Thursday, May 2

This was the next time! Those who attended this game saw perhaps the best quarter, maybe even the best-ever half, ever played by an Old Saybrook girls' lacrosse team. It was twenty-four minutes during which the Rams hardly made a mistake ... not a dropped ball or a bad pass. The Rams' Draw Demons (Ayla, Kendall ...and Amelia with her butterfly net of a stick) snagged 18 of 26 draws, or 70%, closer to 100% during the first half. It was a day when all twelve players on the Old Saybrook team played their very best at the exact same time. Significantly, an increasingly frustrated North Branford team had 28 (minor and major) penalties called on them versus 11 for Old Saybrook.

Claire Cassella was high scorer for the Rams with 3 goals and 3 assists. Kendall Dobratz had 5 goals, while Lila Cadley had 2 goals and 2 assists. Ayla D'Anna scored twice and Amelia Sigersmith and Sylvie Webber had one tally each. Erin Fiorelli had a banner day defending the goal for the Rams with 6 saves.

Lost to Old Lyme 6-14, Saturday, May 4

The Rams were unable to re-create, or recover, the same edge that had enabled Old Saybrook to defeat North Branford 2 days earlier. Old Lyme's Goulding and Antonelli scored 5 goals each against a tentative Rams' defense while in the Rams' goal, Erin Fiorelli still netted an impressive 9 saves.

Ayla D'Anna turned in 3 goals and 2 assists. Kendall Dobratz scored twice while Amelia Sigersmith scored once and Claire Cassella had one assist.

As the Rams did not have a single substitute for this game, Felicia Lombard and Caroline Adams were able to play an entire game against a worthy opponent... an opportunity to build for the future...possibly even for later on during the present season.

With four games remaining (all Shoreline League), Old Saybrook has a good chance to play in the shoreline championship...an opportunity to face both Old Lyme and North Branford once again. This week, the Rams face Haddam-Killingworth on Tuesday, at 4:00, and Morgan (Clinton) at 7:00, both away.

For the coaches

Coach Dick Shriver

Girls' Varsity Lacrosse...Week # 6 ending May 12, 2024

League record	W - 7	L–3
Overall	W–8	L–6

Beat Haddam-Killingworth 14–13, Tuesday, May 7

It was a hot day for lacrosse...and the game reflected the heat. Nonetheless, Old Saybrook took an early lead and held on to a narrow margin throughout the game. Kendall Dobratz registered a season-high of 6 goals plus an assist. Claire Cassella was in second place with 3 goals and 1 assist. Amelia Sigersmith had 1 goal and 4 assists while Lila Cadley had 3 scores. Ayla D'Anna scored once and assisted twice. Erin Fiorelli started in the goal and had 2 saves; Cali Morelli had five saves.

Beat Morgan 12–8

This night game in Clinton was a thriller for Old Saybrook. It was the second game this season in which the entire Rams team played hard and well, from start to finish, with plenty of noise. The "Draw Demons" of Ayla D'Anna, Kendall Dobratz and Amelia Sigersmith dominated at the draw and scored on a high percentage of opportunities. Co-captain Grace Desmond led her defensive cadre to stop the aggressive Morgan team in its tracks time and again, take the ball away, and then execute clears that proceeded from one quick, crisp pass, to another, all the way up the field; on one occasion, Ainsley Sigersmith raced the ball the length of the field into relative safety behind the opponent's goal. Rams goalie Cali Morelli is credited with 9 saves.

On offense, co-captain Ayla D'Anna led with 5 goals and 4 assists and many clearing passes and runs. Kendall Dobratz retrieved her share of loose balls at the center draw and tallied another 5 goals and 1 assist. Lila Cadley and co-captain Amelia Sigersmith scored one goal apiece.

Next Week: The Rams end their regular season as they face Cromwell on Tuesday evening at 7:00 and Valley Regional at 6:30 Wednesday evening, both at home; on Wednesday evening, the team and school will honor the Rams' lone senior, Amelia Sigersmith...as well as Valley's lone senior, and long-time respected competitor, Rowen Pilon.

Girls' Varsity Lacrosse...Week #7 ending May 25, 2024

Regular Season:

League record	W - 9	L–3
Overall	W–10	L–6

Post Season:
    Shoreline League Semi-Final

Old Saybrook 8...North Branford 10

In the two regular-season games between these two rivals, North Branford won the first game by one goal, and Old Saybrook won the second game by four goals. Both teams seemed hyped for their third meeting this season. North Branford's "Player of the Year" however, Keana Criscuolo, proved she was worthy of the title by scoring 5 goals and assisting on 4 of the remaining 5 goals. Meanwhile, the Rams struggled with the referees, alleged taunts from the other team, and themselves; coaches found themselves pondering their share of mistakes. In the post-game review, the team did some soul-searching to pump themselves back up for the State playoffs by learning and re-learning the life lesson that positive attitudes can be contagious...but that negative attitudes can be even more contagious; that there is no place in a team sport for a discouraging word; that even a goldfish knows it's best to quickly forget a dropped ball or bad pass.

With the Rams leading by two goals less than two minutes before the half, the thunderbirds evened the score, 5 all, by halftime; they held on to the momentum to win, 10–8. For the Rams, Lila Cadley was high scorer with 3 goals, Claire Cassella had 2, while Ayla D'Anna had 1 goal and, importantly, 4 assists. Ainsley and Amelia Sigersmith had 1 goal apiece. In the goal, Cali Morelli registered 11 saves, or better than 50%.

With any luck, Old Saybrook will meet North Branford again in the State playoffs which begin Tuesday, May 28. The pairings should be published momentarily.

For the coaches,

Dick Shriver

Girls' Varsity Lacrosse...Week #8 ending June 1, 2024

Regular Season:

League record	W - 9		L–3
Overall	W–10		L–6

Post Season:

Shoreline League Semi-Final
Old Saybrook 8...North Branford 10

States...Round of Sixteen
Old Saybrook 13 .... Wheeler 15

Thirty-two practices and seventeen games into the season the Old Saybrook Girls' Varsity Lacrosse Team had improved greatly and was up for what turned out to be the final game of the season. Having beaten every team in the Shoreline League except Old Lyme which, in the event, lost to North Branford in the championship round, the Rams had a good chance to advance in the States playoffs. Alas, it was not to be. Wheeler took a 6–1 lead early on. Old Saybrook got its act together and went ahead 11–10 in the third quarter. In the end, Wheeler's star player, Sophia Gouveia tallied for 8 goals and 2 assists.

Kendall Dobratz turned in a stunning game with 6 goals and 1 assist, and extraordinary field play throughout. In a fine display of team leadership, Ayla D"Anna turned up the heat with 3 goals and 4 assists. Lila Cadley, a competitor to the end, scored twice. In her last game for Old Saybrook, senior Amelia Sigersmith, a consistent snagger of ground balls throughout the season, scored once and assisted once. Freshman Sylvie Webber, in a sign of things to come, scored the opening goal for Old Saybrook. In the goal, Cali Morelli had 14 saves for, once again, an average of 50%.

The three co-captains, Amelia, Ayla and Grace Desmond, should be proud of what their team accomplished this year: a regular season record of 9 wins–3 losses with a squad of 15 that included 8 freshmen. 2024 was an important and satisfying building year for Old Saybrook.

Special thanks to Hilary Sigersmith for such an excellent job of score-keeping for the entire season.

For the Coaches: Dick Shriver

Appendix B
Letters on Behalf of Students

I always felt privileged to be asked to write letters of recommendation (mostly to colleges) on behalf of our players. They had so many options other than a coach. However, the time they spent on the lacrosse field could be turned into recommendations concerning character. Here are some examples:

Letter of Recommendation for Carrington Hartt

To Whom It May Concern:

I have been Head Lacrosse Coach of the Girls' Varsity Lacrosse Team at the Old Saybrook High School for all of Carrington's high school years (cut short this past spring because of COVID-19). Carrington has the character, ability, and personality to be an outstanding person in sport, college, career, and life.

I have known Carrington mainly as her lacrosse coach.

Carrington was a starting player as a high school freshman in 2018. She was third high scorer that season with 23 goals and 15 assists. The following year, Carrington's record included 39 goals and 24 assists. She mainly played at the midfield, taking the center draw on many occasions. Of all the players on the field, Carrington was the one to take a leadership role in what to do in difficult situations. She has been a great leader by example.

I am quoting here from my writeup (for the parents) of the game in the spring of 2019, Old Saybrook against Branford: "The hard work in a competitive lacrosse game is done largely in the not-so-glamorous trenches of ground balls, interceptions, good clearing runs and passes downfield, and ball control in place of mistakes under pressure and their inevitable consequences, mayhem. Such positive outcomes are largely the result of combining intensity and alertness 100.00% of the time with a cool head, at top speed. Sophomore Midfielder Gilly [aka Carrington] Hartt put all these together and then some in the Rams' Saturday triumph over Branford." Old Saybrook won that day, 16–10.

As a sophomore, Carrington made the Second Team, All-State, and First Team, All Shoreline (local League). As a senior this coming spring, I'm confident she will be a strong leader of her team.

Carrington is a thinking player. When the going gets tough, she can and does settle her team down. When the going gets tough, she can excel. When the going gets tough, I will look to Carrington to be the best spokesperson for her teammates, and for what's going on out on the field.

Outside of lacrosse, I have to lean on Carrington's resume. Her academic and other extracurricular volunteer activities are no surprise, however, and to me, speak for themselves. She has the energy and inclination to serve others in meaningful ways. Her potential in all things seems to have no limits. I am very pleased to recommend Carrington Hartt to any college or institution to which she may apply, and would be happy to answer any questions.

Richard H. Shriver
Head Coach Girls' Varsity Lacrosse
Old Saybrook High School, CT
rhsusa@gmail.com
860-671-1634

Letter of Recommendation for Ayla D'Anna's Application to the National Honor Society

To Whom It May Concern:

October 16, 2023

I have known Ayla D'Anna for the past two years as head coach of the Old Saybrook girls' lacrosse team. During these two seasons, Ayla grew and improved in so many ways, demonstrating her capacity to transfer learning and experience into solid personal and team accomplishments. Her team won the Shoreline League championship in both seasons, and in the spring of 2023, Ayla's personal and permanent record included 32 goals, 13 assists and earned her an honorable mention in the Shoreline League.

My personal and favorite recollections of Ayla as a sophomore in high school (the season of 2023) turn to this: at moments of truth in the heat of battle, Ayla is 100% focused and poised to do exactly the right thing with split-second timing; she proved this time and again in 2023 with a pass to the right teammate at precisely the right time, or a rifle-accurate scoring shot under extreme pressure. She can think and act in the midst of intense chaos around her. This is not a trait one can coach; this is something inside the player that a coach can only wish for.

Ayla is outwardly friendly, humble, and reserved. She has a good sense of humor and does not take life too seriously. She is well-liked and respected by her teammates and coaches. On top of all this, and somewhat surprisingly given her outwardly calm demeanor, she is a formidable competitor, with potential for great leadership in her future.

As a three-sport athlete, Ayla manages her time well. She volunteers for a number of community activities both in school and in her town. It is my great pleasure to support Ayla's application for membership in the National Honor Society.

Richard H. Shriver
Head Coach, Girls' Varsity Lacrosse
Old Saybrook High School
860-671-1634

Letter of recommendation for Laura Day, Junior at Old Saybrook High School, CT

To Whom It May Concern:

I have known Laura for some years now as her lacrosse coach, initially in the youth league, and this past season, 2021, when Laura played varsity lacrosse as a sophomore at Old Saybrook, High School.

In the 2021 season, Laura improved steadily throughout the season in several important ways: self-confidence, team play, and acceptance by her teammates. By mid-season, she started at midfield. In this position, she was effective on defense as well as offense. Laura thinks on her feet in the heat of battle. She is fast, highly competitive, and an inspiration to her teammates. During the regular season, Laura finished with 29 goals and 8 assists, and was third high scorer on the team…as a sophomore.

Laura is a natural leader, a role she fills with humility. She takes initiative. She is not afraid to express herself to suggest where team play and performance can be improved. She has excellent judgment about important matters. She has an adult, mature, gentle way of expressing herself, of making her arguments, which means she is persuasive and effective in bringing about positive change.

Laura's academic record speaks for itself (e.g., A's in three AP courses plus two honors courses). She has also been a volunteer coach in the youth lacrosse program. To me, these facts are clear indications that Laura knows herself well, and knows how to manage herself to excel in the classroom, on the athletic field, and in her community.

For these reasons, I am pleased and proud to recommend Laura Day for recognition by the National Honor Society.

I would be pleased to respond to any questions.

Richard H. Shriver
Head Coach
Girls' Varsity Lacrosse Team
Old Saybrook High School
Old Saybrook, CT
860-671-1634

This letter is written on behalf of Cali B. Morelli in support of her college applications

To whom it may concern:

I have known Cali for the past three years as head coach of the Girls' Varsity Lacrosse team at Old Saybrook High School. Cali played goalie, was second string her freshman year, and was our starting goalie the past two seasons. Just being a goalie in the first instance is a sign of character; one has to be willing, and train oneself, to try to stop a hard ball thrown at you with all possible force, by getting your stick or any part of your anatomy, in the path of the ball…without regard for your personal safety…just the opposite of one's instincts for self-preservation. Goalies are special. Cali is special.

Cali is an outstanding athlete as demonstrated by her performance as a champion cheerleader and starting goalie in lacrosse. She is both disciplined and coachable. She is eager to "do better" at all times, and seeks relevant advice from her coaches. She is a very good individual player and a fine team player, encouraging her teammates at all times. Cali was our starting goalie in the spring of 2023 when her team won the Shoreline League Championship. Cali does her best at all times, and is a good leader by example.

Cali's prowess as a scholar-athlete is exemplified by being a member of the National Honor Society; her extra-curricular pursuits and activities as a member of her community also speak for themselves as she is, currently, a junior firefighter with the Old Saybrook (CT) Fire Department, again, willing to put herself in harms' way not only for her teammates, but also for her community.

While always eager to excel, Cali is, by nature, easy-going, friendly and outgoing. As a former coach and teacher at one of the service academies, I can attest that Cali is an excellent candidate for any of the service academies.

Richard H. Shriver
Head Coach, Girls' Varsity Lacrosse (ending in 2024)
Old Saybrook High School
869-671-1634

Appendix C
Dick Shriver's History as Lacrosse Coach and Player

As a coach:
1960: Coach of the Ohio State University freshman lacrosse team
1974-1975: Founder and coach of the Mountain Lakes (NJ) high school lacrosse program
2006-2007: Coach of the Berlin (Germany) Victoria Men's Club Lacrosse Team. Victoria won the championship of Eastern Germany in 2006.
2008: Assistant coach of the US Coast Guard Academy Women's Lacrosse Team
2009-2011: Head coach, US Coast Guard Academy Women's Lacrosse Team
2012-2014: Head coach, Williams School Girls' Varsity Lacrosse
2015-2017: Coach of girls' youth lacrosse, one season as a certified HS lacrosse referee
2018-2024: Head coach, Girls' Varsity Lacrosse, Old Saybrook (CT) High School
2021: Undefeated in the regular season of the Shoreline League 2022: Shoreline League Champions 2023: Shoreline League Champions

As a player:
1942-1946: Player at St. Paul's School in Mount Washington (Baltimore)
1947: Player on first Middlesex School (Concord, MA) lacrosse team, appointed captain by the coach as the only student who had prior experience as a player
1948-1949: Player and captain (elected) of the Middlesex School lacrosse team
1950: Player on Middlesex School lacrosse team

1951: Player and captain (elected) of the Middlesex School lacrosse team, ranked number three in New England

1952: Elected co-captain of Cornell University freshman lacrosse team

1953–1955: Player on Cornell University Varsity lacrosse team, elected captain in 1955, played on North Team in the 1955 North-South championship game. Honorable mention All-American, 1954 and 1955. Awarded the Lawrence Van Buren Woodworth Lacrosse Trophy, *Given in memory by his friends to the player who most exemplifies competitive spirit and fair play.*

Dick Shriver had the most points scored (goals plus assists) for Cornell's varsity in 1953, 1954, and 1955.

In their book, *The Lacrosse Story*, Alexander M. Weyand and Milton R. Roberts state, on page 208 of the summary for 1955, "Dick Shriver of Cornell totaled 5 goals and 9 assists against Colgate for a single game high."

www.ingramcontent.com/pod-product-compliance
Lightning Source LLC
Chambersburg PA
CBHW051214090426
42742CB00022B/3457